TASTY

PHOTOGRAPHY BY TAMARA WEST

CHELSEA WINTER

# TASTY

ALLEN&UNWIN
AUCKLAND • SYDNEY • MELBOURNE • LONDON

**For Andrea**

You are, quite simply, the best. I love you and believe in you more than you could know.

# CONTENTS

# WELCOME

Hello, my beloved readers. Oh, how I've missed you!

A lot has happened since I first started writing *Tasty* back in 2021. I had another baby. Moved cities. Transitioned from a romantic relationship into a co-parenting one, while holding awareness and intention throughout the process. Grew my hair longer. Started a big garden and had to learn how to look after it. Turned 40. Started figuring out who Chelsea Winter really is. Let a lot of sh*t go and invited a lot of magical stuff in. Discovered my inner compass, and started to fine-tune it. Learned a lot about ... everything. And began to find the balance in my life again. Now here I am, age 40, mother of two incredible boys, living my dream, sun-kissed and salty and green-thumbed and thriving in Taranaki, beaming happily from the pages of my seventh cookbook. Beside myself with gratitude for all of it. And, as you can see, once more I've decided to focus on brilliant plant-based recipes that the whole family will love.

This next bit might surprise you, though. These days I'm not actually following a fully plant-based diet (you'd call it more of a 'plant-rich' diet, really). So why, then, would I make *Tasty* fully plant-based? The answer is simple (as most good answers are) — it just felt right.

I reckon a good life, at a fundamental level, is found in the joyful art of b a l a n c e. And when it comes to food, balance is especially important. Think about it: the first five bestselling cookbooks I created are packed with the full spectrum of animal protein, but very few vegetarian recipes (and, er, virtually no plant-based ones). Then came *Supergood*, fully plant-based. And now I'm continuing to recalibrate with another sumptuous stack of life-changing, deliciously unexpected plant-based staples. Inspiration is needed now more than ever — that much is evident.

And guess what else? This time I've decided to give highly refined sugar the heave-ho, too. My sprogs, Sage and Sky, don't do well on it (no child does), so I don't really use it at the moment. In my experience, other less-refined sugars can be much gentler — and that means we tend to avoid that giddying high followed by the hideous crash. I actually feel much better for it, too. It just makes sense.

I realise that what one chooses to eat is an incredibly personal and ever-changing journey, and I don't believe there's a 'right' or 'wrong' way to do it. So, it's my intention that this book will be used in different ways depending on who's using it — and it really does cater for everyone.

For the millions of you who cook every day for loved ones with allergies or intolerances to eggs, dairy or gluten, allow me to present more than 80 fabulous recipes that you can serve safely, knowing they'll be happily devoured. A tonne of you will be relieved (like me) to be baking goodies that aren't crammed with refined sugar but still taste like those nostalgic treats we all know and love. Those among you enjoying a vegan or vegetarian lifestyle will obviously be chuffed once again, as *Tasty* is a legitimate treasure trove of beautiful, flavour-packed, easy-to-follow recipes that are good for the animals, the planet and our bodies. The same goes for those needing inspiration for the odd meat-free meal that the whole family (even the staunchest carnie) will love — too easy!

On the other hand, many of my beloved home cooks will choose to serve meat or sustainably-caught fish in (or alongside) my recipes. Maybe you'll garnish a stir-fry with a crispy free-range fried egg. Some of you will use regular cheese, butter or cream instead of the dairy-free variants, where and when it works for you. Some of you will sub in regular sugar if you don't have what's specified on hand.

**You guys do you — it's all good with me.**

I'll be here, time and time again, to provide ridiculously tasty recipes, carefully and scrupulously crafted with pure joy, integrity and discernment, especially for you. I wholeheartedly love what I do and I'm beyond grateful that I get to do it — I hope you can feel that vibe on every page, with every mouthful.

So now go, my friends, and follow your hearts. Make the recipes your own. Enjoy the journey, make a mess (or don't), have a laugh, gather the people you love close, often. Cook for happiness — because, in the end, it will always be about that for me. And may *Tasty* become a familiar, tatty, grubby part of your kitchen as it helps you find balance — with your food, in your life, for your soul.

I'm sending every one of you sooo much effing love.
You bunch of rock stars.

Chelsea

# MAINS

# ALOO PALAK

**PREP** 20 minutes
**COOK** 45 minutes
**SERVES** 4–5

- 250g (9 oz) spinach, thick stalks removed
- 2½ cups vegetable stock
- 1 tbsp finely julienned fresh ginger
- 1 large green chilli, deseeded and finely chopped
- ⅓ cup chopped fresh coriander
- 3 tbsp olive, grapeseed or sunflower oil
- 2 large onions, thinly sliced
- 4–5 cloves garlic, finely chopped
- 2 tsp mild curry powder
- 2 tsp ground coriander
- 2 tsp ground cumin
- ½ tsp ground cardamom
- 1.25kg (2 lb 12 oz) potatoes, peeled and cut into 3cm (1¼ in) chunks
- 2 tsp vegetable or imitation chicken stock powder
- 2 tsp coconut sugar or maple syrup
- 1 tsp salt
- ½ tsp garam masala
- lemon juice, to taste

**TO SERVE (OPTIONAL)**

- cooked rice
- naan, roti or pappadums
- coconut yoghurt
- tamarind chutney
- fresh coriander

Aloo palak (translated as 'potato spinach') has of late been one of my favourite curries to order from an Indian takeout. (I still dream about a late-night one I devoured in Greytown after a book event there. Who'd have thought?) It looks simple here, but there are loads of ways to approach this dish and it took me ages to perfect the recipe so it felt balanced with the right level of spices, creaminess and spinachyness — and with good sauce texture. I'm in love with the result — the garam masala and fresh pop of ginger added at the end lift the whole thing heavenward. Plus, any main meal with potatoes as the star ingredient is a winner in my eyes. It tastes even better the next day, although you may need to add a touch more water to thin it down. Bonus — both my kids love this!

Steam or simmer the spinach for 1–2 minutes until wilted and tender. Rinse in a colander under cold water until cool. Place in a blender or bullet with the stock, half the ginger, half the green chilli and the fresh coriander. Whizz until silky smooth. Set aside.

Heat the oil in a large casserole dish or deep pan over a medium-low heat. Add the onions and cook, stirring frequently, for 10–15 minutes until soft and golden. Add the garlic and remaining chilli and cook for another couple of minutes.

Add the curry powder, ground coriander, cumin and cardamom and a splash of water and stir for another minute or two until you have a nice fragrant mush.

Add the spinach mixture, potatoes, stock powder, coconut sugar or maple syrup and salt. Stir to combine, then cover with a lid (leaving a small gap) and simmer over a medium-low heat for about 30 minutes until the potatoes are tender. If you think it needs more liquid, add a little more water. If you think it looks too runny when the potatoes are cooked, simmer it with the lid off for a bit.

Stir in the garam masala and the remaining ginger. Check the flavours and add salt, pepper and/or lemon juice until it tastes balanced to you.

Serve over cooked rice with your choice of naan, roti or pappadums, coconut yoghurt, chutney and/or extra coriander.

## TIPS & SWAPS

- It's fine to swap some or all of the spinach for silverbeet or chard (be sure to weigh it after discarding the white stems), just remember it will take a little longer to wilt. Alternatively, you can use 150g (5½ oz) frozen spinach instead of the fresh spinach. You don't need to steam it — just defrost it then squeeze out the water.
- Use 2 green chillies if you like it slightly spicier.

# TERIYAKI-GLAZED TOFU CHUNKS

**PREP** 20 minutes
**COOK** 30 minutes
**SERVES** 4

800g (1 lb 12 oz) firm tofu (I prefer organic)
⅔ cup cornflour and/or rice flour
peanut oil or other neutral oil

**SAUCE**

¾ cup water
½ cup soy sauce or tamari
¼ cup coconut sugar
1½ tbsp cornflour mixed with 2 tbsp water to make a slurry
1 tbsp peanut or grapeseed oil
1 tbsp rice wine vinegar or white vinegar
1 tbsp finely grated fresh ginger
4–5 cloves garlic, crushed
1 tsp toasted sesame oil
¼ tsp five-spice powder
¼ tsp fine black pepper
¼ tsp fine white pepper

**TO SERVE**

cooked rice or noodles
finely chopped spring onion, chives and/or coriander
toasted sesame seeds (optional)

Winner, winner teriyaki dinner! This wondrous sauce would make anything taste good, and my homemade version isn't loaded with white sugar, preservatives and god knows what else. Just a whole lotta good-quality ingredients that really mean business, especially when they're working together. Once you try it you may never go back. The teriyaki works superbly here, coating chunks of perfectly fried crispy tofu, which makes such a great textural canvas for the intense Asian flavours we're bringing. Have all the garnish and other meal components ready to go before you start cooking the tofu, because the tofu is best served freshly fried so it doesn't go soggy. Serve with your favourite Asian greens, slaw or salad.

To make the teriyaki sauce, place all the ingredients in a small saucepan over a medium heat. Stir constantly for a few minutes until it starts to thicken up. Allow it to simmer for a minute once it's thickened, then remove from the heat and set aside.

To prepare the tofu, tear or cut it into bite-sized chunks and place it in a heatproof bowl. Cover with just-boiled water and soak for 5 minutes. Drain in a colander.

Place half the cornflour and/or rice flour in a medium bowl. Add half the tofu and toss to coat evenly until most of the flour is stuck to the tofu. Transfer to a small roasting tray or large plate and repeat with the remaining flour and tofu.

Heat ¼ cup oil in a pan over a medium-high heat. When hot, add half the tofu and leave to fry until one side is turning golden and crispy. It won't go as golden brown as usual because of the flour, but it will get super crispy even if it doesn't look like it. Carefully turn each piece until it's crispy all over.

Transfer to a plate lined with a couple of paper towels or to a wire rack sitting over paper towels and repeat with the remaining tofu.

Before serving, reheat the teriyaki sauce in the saucepan if needed – you may need to add a little more water. Toss the hot fried tofu through the warm sauce. Serve atop rice or noodles, garnished with spring onion, chives and/or coriander and sesame seeds (if using).

### TIPS & SWAPS

- If you want more sauce, you can add half as much again of all the ingredients except the garlic.

# MOROCCAN LENTIL SOUP

**PREP** 20 minutes, plus 6+ hours soaking time
**COOK** 30 minutes
**SERVES** 4

Soup just got flash. This recipe is so very special, so very authentic and truly a celebration of magical, wondrous Moroccan flavours in a bowl. Best of all, it's easy to put together and have sitting ready to go when you need it. Once you've got the lusciously spiced soup singing with fresh herbs, drizzled with spectacular chermoula and festooned with sweet dates and tart preserved lemon (promise me you'll find preserved lemon), it's honestly a soup-eating experience like no other. I rush to serve it when I have guests – and I'm not usually a soup-server, especially not for the main course. Do me a favour and try it. You'll be pleased you did.

- 1 red onion, quartered
- 2 stalks celery, roughly chopped
- 4 cloves garlic, peeled
- 3 tbsp extra virgin olive oil
- ¾ cup puy-style green lentils, rinsed
- ½ cup split red lentils, rinsed
- 4 cups vegetable or imitation chicken stock
- 600g (1 lb 5 oz) passata or canned crushed tomatoes
- ½ cup water
- 2 tsp maple syrup or coconut sugar
- 1 tsp salt
- 1 tsp fine black pepper
- 1 cup finely chopped spinach
- ¼ cup finely chopped fresh coriander leaves and stalks
- ¼ cup finely chopped flat-leaf parsley
- 1 tbsp lemon juice

**FERMENT**

- ½ cup warm water
- 2 tbsp flour, rice flour or fine semolina
- 2 tbsp lemon juice

**SPICE MIX**

- 2 tsp ground coriander
- 1½ tsp smoked paprika
- 1 tsp ground cumin
- 1 tsp ground turmeric
- ½ tsp paprika
- ¼ tsp ground cinnamon
- ¼ tsp ground ginger

**TO SERVE (OPTIONAL)**

- chermoula (see page 218) or extra chopped herbs
- 5–6 dates, finely chopped
- rind of 2 preserved lemon wedges, finely diced, or zest of 1 lemon

To make the ferment, combine the ingredients in a small bowl and leave overnight, or for at least 6 hours (it doesn't need to bubble).

To make the spice mix, combine the ingredients in a small bowl.

To make the soup, place the onion, celery and garlic in a food processor and pulse until you have a coarse chunky chop. If you don't have a food processor, just finely chop it all.

Heat the oil in a large saucepan, add the onion, celery and garlic and stir constantly over a medium heat for about 5 minutes, adding a little water if it starts to stick.

Add the spice mix and cook, stirring, for about 2 minutes until fragrant. Again, you can add a little water if it seems dry.

Add both kinds of lentils and the stock. Simmer, uncovered, over a medium heat for about 15 minutes, stirring a few times.

Add the passata or canned tomatoes, water and ferment mixture and simmer for about 7 minutes, stirring occasionally. If the lentils aren't quite cooked, add a little more water, cover and simmer until they are.

Stir in the maple syrup or coconut sugar, salt and pepper.

Just before serving, add the spinach, fresh coriander, parsley and lemon juice. Simmer for another couple of minutes just to heat through and wilt the spinach. If you'd like it a bit thinner, add more water.

Check the flavours and adjust the salt, pepper, lemon juice and coconut sugar or maple syrup until it tastes balanced to you. It kind of depends on how salty your stock was and how peppery you want it (I'm pepper-obsessed).

To serve, ladle the soup into serving bowls. Top each with your choice of a 1–2 tbsp dollop of chermoula or extra herbs, a sprinkle of dates and a little preserved lemon or lemon zest.

**TIPS & SWAPS**

- The ferment gives a beautiful tang and thickens the soup. Ideally you'll let it sit for at least 6 hours, but if you can't wait, it will still be nice even if you just leave it 15 minutes.
- Kids probably don't need the chermoula as the soup is tasty enough without it.

# NOODLY PEANUT STIR-FRY

**PREP** 20 minutes
**COOK** 20 minutes
**SERVES** 4–5

Everyone loves a good noodle stir-fry, and it's the creamy peanut sauce that makes this one special (it nearly feels like a pad thai). Never again will you need to reach for a jar of store-bought stir-fry sauce! Well, you probably still will, but at least you have this one up your sleeve now. I've kept the veges simple because it's easy to get carried away with an avalanche of different things in a stir-fry but sometimes less is more — and much easier to prepare, too. Make sure you prep all the veges before you start cooking. If tofu isn't your thing, you can sear your choice of protein in its place and add it at the end.

- 200g (7 oz) dried or 400g (14 oz) fresh noodles
- 300g (10½ oz) firm tofu
- neutral oil, such as peanut, grapeseed or sunflower, for frying
- 1 onion, thinly sliced
- 3 carrots, julienned into thin strips
- 5 cups (about 400g / 14 oz) green or savoy cabbage, thinly sliced
- 2–3 spring onions, white and green parts separated and finely chopped
- ½ cup chopped fresh chives or coriander
- ⅓ cup roasted peanuts, roughly chopped
- chilli oil (optional)

**SAUCE**

- ⅓ cup crunchy peanut butter
- ⅓ cup soy sauce or tamari
- 4 cloves garlic, crushed
- 1 tbsp cornflour mixed with 2 tbsp water to make a slurry
- 1 tbsp coconut sugar
- 2 tsp vegetable stock powder
- 2 tsp rice wine vinegar or white vinegar
- 2 tsp sesame oil
- 2 tsp sriracha or small pinch chilli flakes or ½ fresh chilli, chopped finely
- 1 tsp salt

To make the sauce, place the ingredients in a jug or bowl and stir to combine. Set aside.

If using dried noodles, cook according to the packet directions then drain, setting aside ⅓ cup of the cooking water to use later. If using fresh noodles, soak in a bowl of just-boiled water for 2 minutes before draining and setting aside the water. If your noodles are the super-long type, you could lay them out on a clean board and make one cut across to halve them — it makes stir-frying easier later. Up to you!

Crumble the tofu into small pieces and press firmly in a clean, dry tea towel to absorb the excess moisture.

Heat 2 tbsp oil in a wok over a high heat. When shimmering, carefully add the tofu (watch for splatters!). Leave to fry until golden brown on the bottom, then stir and repeat until it's golden brown all over (it may take a wee while). Season well with salt and pepper, then set aside in a bowl.

Add another 2 tbsp oil to the wok over a high heat. Add the onion and cook for a couple of minutes until fragrant and turning golden. Add the carrots and stir-fry for another few minutes. Add the cabbage and white parts of the spring onions and cook again, tossing frequently, until tender. (I use two of my wooden Wonder Spoons — they are perfect for tossing stir-fries.)

Add the noodles and stir-fry for a minute or two to heat through.

Lower the heat to medium-low, then stir in the sauce and the reserved noodle water. Cook for another few minutes until piping hot.

Stir in the green parts of the spring onions and the chives or coriander, reserving a little of each for the garnish. Stir in the peanuts.

To serve, use tongs to transfer the noodles to bowls and then garnish with the reserved spring onion and herbs. Those who love a spicy number can drizzle a little chilli oil on top.

## TIPS & SWAPS

- If you're a fan of red capsicum, you can add one, finely sliced. Or use finely sliced mushrooms.
- Omit or halve the sriracha or chilli if you want it very mild.
- If you're into eggs, a fried free-range organic egg on top would be a yummy addition.
- You can find good chilli oils at the supermarket.

# EASY MASSAMAN

**PREP** 15 minutes
**COOK** 30 minutes
**SERVES** 4

peanut oil or other neutral oil, for frying
1 cup finely chopped shallots
3 cloves garlic, crushed
3 tbsp mild Thai red curry paste
1½ tsp ground cumin
1½ tsp ground coriander
¼ tsp mixed spice
¼ tsp ground cardamom
¼ tsp ground cinnamon
¼ tsp fine white pepper
2 tbsp water
1½ cups vegetable stock
4 medium waxy potatoes, peeled and cut into 3–4cm (1¼–1½ in) dice
400ml (14 fl oz) coconut milk
2–3 tbsp peanut butter
1 tbsp soy sauce or tamari
1 tbsp coconut sugar
1 tbsp lemongrass paste or 1 stalk, bashed a bit (optional)
2 tsp vegetable stock powder
1 tsp ground turmeric
800g (1 lb 12 oz) firm tofu, torn into 3–4cm (1¼–1½ in) chunks
1–2 tbsp lemon or lime juice
½ tsp salt

**TO SERVE**

cooked jasmine rice
fried shallots and/or chopped roasted peanuts
½ cup roughly chopped fresh coriander or Thai basil
finely sliced fresh red chilli (optional)

This is my take on a traditional Massaman curry, which is a favourite for so many. I've taken a few little shortcuts to make life simpler for us all, but it's a solid recipe and absolutely packed with rich, aromatic flavour. I make no apologies for the slightly lengthy nature of the ingredients list; there are a few spices, which is what makes this curry so special, because it's a fusion of different cuisines, not simply Thai. If you want real depth of flavour and balance, leading to lip-smacking satisfaction (the only way I roll), it's gotta be like this. You'll find all you need at the supermarket and it's super simple to put together. You can sub out the fried tofu for whatever protein you prefer if you want to change it up.

Place 3 tbsp oil in a deep pan or casserole dish over a medium-low heat. Add the shallots and cook, stirring frequently, for about 7 minutes until soft and golden. Add the garlic and cook for another minute.

Add the curry paste, spices and water and stir for a minute until you have a thick, fragrant, mushy paste.

Add the stock and potatoes, cover and simmer over a low heat for 10–15 minutes until the potatoes are tender but not mushy. If you don't have a lid, just simmer until the potatoes are tender – you may need a touch more liquid. Add the coconut milk, peanut butter, soy sauce or tamari, coconut sugar, lemongrass (if using), stock powder and turmeric. Simmer for another 10–15 minutes until reduced slightly to your preferred curry consistency. You can always add more liquid to make it thinner, or keep simmering to make it thicker. Turn off the heat while you fry the tofu.

Press the tofu in a clean, dry tea towel to absorb the excess moisture. Season generously with salt and pepper. Heat 3 tbsp oil in a pan over a medium-high heat and fry the tofu until golden brown and crispy all over. Drain on paper towels.

Stir the lemon or lime juice and salt into the curry. Check the flavours and adjust the salt, pepper, lemon or lime juice and coconut sugar until it tastes balanced to you.

To serve, spoon the curry over cooked rice, then top with the tofu, shallots and/or peanuts, herbs and chilli (if using).

### TIPS & SWAPS

- You can add 2–3 cups roughly chopped spinach to the curry if desired.
- If you like, you can coat the dried and seasoned tofu with cornflour for extra crunch.
- If you can get your hands on fresh or dried makrut (kaffir) lime leaves, add one leaf to the simmering mix and remove before serving. Lime zest is a nice addition, too.
- You can buy fried shallots at the supermarket.
- If you can find tamarind paste, use 1 tbsp of this instead of the lime juice – it goes in with the coconut sugars.
- I use a Massel chicken-style stock cube – one cube is the same as 2 tsp stock powder.

# ROASTED PUMPKIN & SPINACH PASTA

**PREP** 35 minutes
**COOK** 10 minutes
**SERVES** 4–5

One of my best-loved recipes! In winter 2023, my first year in Taranaki, this recipe featured at least once a week in my household, except I often used sautéed kale in place of spinach (which you can absolutely do). It's such a comforting dish it warmed the cockles of my heart on the chilliest of evenings. I sometimes roast the garlic whole along with the pumpkin, but usually I find it more satisfying to sauté it in a pan where I can control the level of cooking. The fresh basil adds something special to the sauce, so I'm grateful you can buy it year-round. If you don't eat cashews, I have an alternative for you in the tips section.

- 1kg (2 lb 4 oz) pumpkin or butternut squash
- 1 tbsp coconut sugar or maple syrup
- extra virgin olive oil
- 4–5 cloves garlic, finely chopped
- 1 tbsp fresh thyme leaves
- 300g (10½ oz) dried pasta of choice
- 250–300g (9–10½ oz) spinach, roughly chopped (discard thick stems)
- 1 tbsp lemon juice

**SAUCE**

- 2½ cups unsweetened plant-based milk (I use soy milk)
- ½ cup roughly chopped cashews
- ⅓ cup nutritional yeast flakes
- 2 tsp vegetable or imitation chicken stock powder
- 1 tsp soy sauce or tamari
- 1 tsp salt
- ¼ tsp fine white pepper
- 12 fresh basil leaves

**TO SERVE**

- 120g (4¼ oz) plant-based bacon, chopped (optional)

Preheat the oven to 190°C (375°F) regular bake and line a roasting tray with baking paper.

Peel and deseed the pumpkin or butternut and cut the flesh into roughly 4cm (1½ in) chunks. Place on the prepared roasting tray and drizzle with the coconut sugar or maple syrup and 3 tbsp oil. Toss to combine, season generously with salt and pepper, then roast for 15–20 minutes, or until golden and tender right through.

Heat 3 tbsp oil in a small saucepan over a medium heat. Add the garlic and let it sizzle gently until just turning golden and fragrant (don't let it get dark, it won't take long). Add the thyme, give it a shake, then immediately transfer everything to a small bowl.

If using the plant-based bacon, fry it in a little olive oil with salt and pepper over a medium heat until very crispy. Set aside.

To make the cashew sauce, place the ingredients in a blender or bullet. Tip in the garlicky oil. Whizz until perfectly smooth — 45 seconds on high in a blender, less in a bullet.

Cook the pasta according to the packet directions, using a large soup pot big enough to hold the whole lot at the end. When it is cooked to your liking (slightly al dente for me), dump in the spinach and cook for a minute to wilt.

Drain the pasta and spinach in a colander and return it to the pot. Pour in the cashew sauce.

Place the pot over a medium-high heat and stir constantly with a wooden spoon until the sauce has thickened. If it gets too thick you can always add more milk (especially if you have to leave it sitting a while before serving).

Lastly, stir in the pumpkin and lemon juice (it's nice when the pumpkin pieces start melting away into the sauce, so don't be afraid to give it a good enthusiastic rustle-up). Check if it needs more salt.

Serve in bowls, topped with the plant-based bacon (if using).

## TIPS & SWAPS

- If your blender isn't overly powerful, you may need to soak the cashews in boiled water for 15–30 minutes first.
- For a nut-free sauce, simmer 3 cups plant-based cream with a slurry of 2 tbsp cornflour and 2 tbsp water until thickened up like a pasta sauce. Whisk in the remaining sauce ingredients (finely chop the basil) and add to the drained pasta, spinach and pumpkin.
- I use a Massel chicken-style stock cube — one cube is the same as 2 tsp stock powder.
- You can add a simple green salad and garlic bread on the side to fancy it up.

# MEATBALLS & GRAVY

**PREP** 40 minutes
**COOK** 20 minutes
**SERVES** 4

### MEATBALLS

½ cup uncooked brown rice
1 tbsp vegetable stock powder
¾ cup (20g / ¾ oz) dried mushrooms
¾ cup walnuts
¾ cup textured soy protein (see page 227)
2 tsp soy sauce or tamari
¾ cup just-boiled water
⅓ cup tapioca flour or gluten-free flour blend (see page 222)
2 tbsp tomato paste
2 tsp white (shiro) miso paste
2 tsp smoked paprika
2 tsp finely chopped fresh rosemary
¾ tsp fine black pepper
¾ tsp salt
2 tbsp olive oil

### GRAVY

¼ cup flour or 3 tbsp gluten-free flour blend (see page 222)
2 cups vegetable or imitation chicken or beef stock
3 tbsp nutritional yeast flakes
3 tbsp plant-based butter or refined coconut oil
2 tsp soy sauce or tamari
1½ tsp Vegemite or Marmite
1 small clove garlic, crushed
½ tsp porcini powder
¼ tsp mustard powder or ½ tsp dijon mustard
⅛ tsp fine white pepper
⅛ tsp fine black pepper

I've struggled for years to find a meat-free meatball that has decent texture and bite to it. I simply cannot abide mushy meatballs (or mushy burger patties, for that matter – they get my hackles up). Finally, a few brilliant ingredients that you may not have cooked with before have come together in this recipe to fulfil my heart's desire and nail the brief. I love devouring these with sautéed cabbage and mashed potatoes, slathered in the gravy, of course. They're easy-as to make. You may have to source the dried mushrooms at a specialty food store, greengrocer or Asian supermarket, but everything else will be at your local supermarket. For Christmas, I make a double batch of the meatballs and gravy and bake them all together in one dish for maximum impact.

To make the meatballs, cook the rice for about 5 minutes less than the packet directions until tender but still with a little bite, adding the stock powder to the cooking water. Drain well, then allow to cool until it is just warm. Whizz in a food processor until gluggy but with some texture, so the grains of rice are mostly half the original size. Set aside.

Soak the dried mushrooms in water until soft enough to chop (this will take 10 minutes for slices or longer for whole mushrooms). Drain, then place in a food processor along with the walnuts and pulse until you have a chunky crumb – not a purée!

Place the soy protein in a large mixing bowl with the soy sauce or tamari. Pour the boiled water over the top, stir and allow to soak for 5 minutes. Season with salt and pepper.

Add the rice mixture, walnut mixture, flour, tomato paste, miso, paprika, rosemary, pepper and salt. Stir well to combine evenly.

Using clean, damp hands, roll the mixture into walnut-sized balls. If not cooking immediately, they can be refrigerated in a sealed container for up to 48 hours until you're ready to cook them.

To make the gravy, place the flour in a small bowl with 3 tbsp of the stock and mix to a slurry. Transfer to a small saucepan with the remaining stock and all the remaining ingredients and whisk to combine.

Stir over a medium heat for about 5 minutes, or until thickened and smooth. Check the flavours and season with salt if you think it needs it. Cover until needed. To reheat, you may need to add a little more water to thin it down.

When you're ready to cook the meatballs, preheat the oven to 180°C (350°F) regular bake.

Heat the olive oil in a pan over a medium heat and fry the meatballs in batches until browned all over. Transfer to a roasting tray and bake for 15 minutes to cook out the flour. You can choose to pour the gravy over the top while they bake, or add it hot at the end when you serve them up.

### TIPS & SWAPS

- Refined coconut oil is a flavourless oil that's able to tolerate high heat. It might be labelled 'coconut cooking oil' at the supermarket.
- I love having porcini powder on hand to add amazing flavour to dishes like this. Just ½ tsp will do the trick.

# GLUTEN-FREE PIZZA

**PREP** 15 minutes, plus 1 hour rising time

**COOK** 25 minutes

**MAKES** 2 small/medium pizzas

As far as gluten-free pizza bases go, this is pretty darned good and it's not tricky to make at all — except don't expect it to behave like regular pizza dough. Ideally you need a stand mixer to churn it up, but a food processor with the blunt dough blade works too — or even the metal blade at a pinch. With this base you still get chewiness and the crusts puff up for a little added crunch. *Bellissimo!*

### DOUGH

- ¾ cup warm water (use 1 cup if using my gluten-free flour blend)
- 1½ tbsp active yeast granules (check expiry date)
- 1 tsp coconut sugar or maple syrup
- 1½ cups gluten-free flour blend (see page 222 or use store-bought)
- ¼ cup tapioca flour or arrowroot flour
- 1 tsp xanthan gum (see page 227)
- ½ tsp salt
- 1½ tbsp extra virgin olive oil

### SAUCE

- ⅓ cup tomato paste
- 3 tbsp water
- 1 tbsp extra virgin olive oil
- 1 large clove garlic, crushed
- 1 tsp dried oregano
- 1 tsp coconut sugar
- ½ tsp salt
- ¼ tsp fine black pepper

### TOPPINGS (OPTIONAL)

- sliced tomatoes or cherry tomatoes (season with salt and drain on paper towels)
- grated cheese (plant-based if preferred)
- fresh plant-based mozzarella (squeeze out excess water)
- dried oregano, fresh basil or pesto
- chilli flakes or cracked pepper
- extra virgin olive oil or truffle oil

### TIPS & SWAPS

- If doubling the recipe, use only an extra 1 tbsp yeast.
- As toppings, you could also try thinly sliced mushrooms, onion and capsicum — or pre-roasted veg.

To make the dough, place the warm water, yeast and coconut sugar or maple syrup in a bowl and whisk briskly for 5 seconds. Set aside for 5–10 minutes until the yeast 'blooms' (goes a bit puffy and rises to the top).

Place the flours, xanthan gum, salt and oil in the bowl of a stand mixer or food processor. Add the frothy yeast mixture and beat on a medium speed with the paddle attachment or whizz in the food processor with the blunt dough blade until everything forms a ball. If you need to, you can add a little more water.

Turn the speed up and keep beating for a good 2–3 minutes until it stops being a ball and starts looking a bit like whipped putty (or tile grout as someone once pointed out!). At this point it won't feel like regular pizza dough, but that's okay.

Lightly grease a medium bowl with a little olive oil. Using an oiled spatula and lightly oiled hands, scrape the dough out of the mixer or food processor, shape it into a rough ball and place it in the greased bowl. Cover and leave somewhere draught-free (the turned-off oven with a bowl of just-boiled water always works for me, or a hot water cupboard). After about an hour, it will have puffed up a bit — not double in size like normal dough, but maybe half as big again. At this point you can use it, or refrigerate it in a sealed container for up to 3 days until needed.

While the dough is rising, make the tomato sauce by stirring the ingredients together in a bowl. Set aside.

When ready to make your pizzas, preheat the oven to 240°C (475°F) fan bake and place 2 pizza stones (or the thickest baking trays you have) in the lower half of the oven to preheat.

Rip two sheets of baking paper about 35cm (14 in) long. Sprinkle one with a little flour. With lightly oiled hands, break off half the dough, shape it into a disc and press it out onto the floured paper.

Use the heels of your hands to spread it out into a rough circle 20–22cm (8–8½ in) in diameter. Make sure the outer edge is thicker than the middle — this will allow the crust to puff up and go chewy. Use the fingers of both hands to smoosh the edge into a nice shape all the way around.

Repeat with the remaining dough and baking paper.

Carefully slide the untopped bases (still on the paper) onto the preheated pizza stones or trays and bake for 3 minutes.

Remove the bases from the oven and top with tomato sauce and toppings of your choice. Season with salt and pepper or chilli flakes and drizzle with a little olive or truffle oil if desired.

Bake for about 10 minutes until the crust is deep golden brown and the cheeses melted and bubbling. You may need 15 minutes if you have lots of veges on there.

# JUNGLE RICE STIR-FRY

**PREP** 35 minutes
**COOK** 45 minutes
**SERVES** 4

This may just be the king of stir-fries! It delivers a truly impressive bombardment of flavours and textures, so you won't know quite what hit you, especially if you're adding all the optional flourishes before you serve it (which I highly recommend – the nut butter sounds odd but boy is it good!). Instead of frying up tofu chunks, I've made it into a deliciously aromatic savoury fried 'mince' (which is so heavenly, I usually double it). It may look humble and serene in the photo here, but your taste buds are in for an experience.

peanut oil or other neutral oil, for frying
2½ cups cooked brown or white rice
2 onions or 1 onion and 1 leek, chopped
2 stalks celery, finely chopped
1 large carrot, chopped
2 cups small broccoli florets
1 cup chopped green beans
2 cups sliced green cabbage
4 cloves garlic, crushed
⅓ cup Jungle Curry Paste (see page 212)
1½ tsp salt
½ tsp fine black pepper

**TOFU**

300g (10½ oz) firm tofu, crumbled
3 tbsp Jungle Curry Paste (see page 212)
⅓ cup coconut cream

**TO SERVE (OPTIONAL)**

lemon or lime wedges
½ cup chopped roasted peanuts or toasted sesame seeds
½ cup finely chopped coriander leaves and stalks
¼ cup almond or peanut butter or unhulled tahini

To fry the rice, heat 2 tbsp oil in a wok or large pan over a high heat and fry the rice until it's a little browned and toasty. Transfer to a bowl and set aside.

To make the tofu mince, heat another 2 tbsp oil in the same wok or pan over a high heat. Add the crumbled tofu and cook for about 10 minutes until golden all over. Reduce the heat to low, add the Jungle Curry Paste and stir-fry to combine. Stir in the coconut cream, transfer to a bowl and set aside.

To make the stir-fry, heat another 2 tbsp oil in the same wok or pan over a high heat. Add the onions and/or leek and stir-fry for 1–2 minutes until soft. Add the celery, carrot, broccoli and beans and cook, stirring often (I use two wooden spoons) for a few minutes until softened.

Add the cabbage and cook for another few minutes until soft. Add the garlic and cook for another minute until fragrant. Add the Jungle Curry Paste and stir to ensure everything is coated.

Add the rice, salt and pepper to the wok. Stir again to combine.

To serve, spoon the stir-fry into bowls and top with the tofu. If desired, finish with a generous squeeze of lemon or lime juice, a scattering of peanuts or sesame seeds and coriander and a drizzle of nut butter or tahini (you may need to thin it with a little boiled water).

## TIPS & SWAPS

- Have all the veges cut and ready to go before you start cooking.
- The tofu mince can be doubled for a hungry home.
- Leftover rice works well, or make it fresh using about 1¼ cups uncooked rice. If you want to cheat, you could even use packets of precooked brown rice.
- Leftover Jungle Curry Paste can be kept in the fridge in an airtight container for a couple of weeks and used as a base for other curries, or the cauliflower salad on page 126.

# SLOW-ROASTED TOMATO BRUSCHETTA

**PREP** 20 minutes
**COOK** 1 hour 30 minutes
**SERVES** 4 as a snack, side or light meal

- 1 loaf ciabatta or sourdough (a day old is fine)
- good-quality extra virgin olive oil
- 1–2 cloves garlic, peeled and halved crossways
- fresh bocconcini or mozzarella (plant-based if preferred) or avocado

**TOMATOES**

- 500–600g (1 lb 2 oz–1 lb 5 oz) red cherry tomatoes
- 8 cloves garlic, unpeeled
- ¼ cup good-quality extra virgin olive oil
- 1 tbsp balsamic vinegar
- 1 tbsp fresh thyme leaves
- 2 tsp coconut sugar
- 1 tsp salt

**BASIL OIL**

- ½ cup good-quality extra virgin olive oil
- ⅓ cup tightly packed fresh basil leaves
- 1 tsp lemon juice or white wine vinegar

You can't go past a good bruschetta, and this one is extraordinary. It's pronounced 'brew-sketta' and you can roll your 'r' there to be more *bellissimo.* I've stuck to a fairly traditional method here except I've slow-roasted the tomatoes to bring out that luscious ripe summer sweetness. The Basil Oil is an extra step but it adds a little bit of magic, especially if you're serving this up to guests. As with any simple dish, it's the quality of the ingredients that counts – so look for lush, fruity, deep green extra virgin olive oil, ripe in-season tomatoes and good-quality bread (stay away from powdery old baguette! *Mamma mia,* that's French). The avocado option will have Italian nonnas everywhere clutching their pearls, but it's a great cheese substitute if you can't get or don't eat bocconcini or mozzarella. There's so much flavour in this dish that it works as a light dinner just by itself.

To roast the tomatoes, preheat the oven to 130°C (250°F) regular bake and line a small roasting tray with baking paper.

Halve the tomatoes, then place in a bowl with the garlic, olive oil, vinegar, thyme, coconut sugar, salt and a good crack of black pepper. Toss to combine, then pour everything onto the prepared tray. Bake for 1 hour 30 minutes, or until sticky and just starting to caramelise. Leave to cool down to room temperature (they will shrivel a bit).

When the roasted garlic is cool enough to handle, squeeze it out of its skins, chop roughly and add back to the tomatoes.

To make the Basil Oil, place the olive oil, basil, lemon juice or vinegar and a pinch of salt in a small food processor or bullet and whizz until smooth. Set aside in a jar, small bowl or jug until needed.

To make the bruschetta, preheat the oven grill to medium-high. Cut the bread into 1.5cm (⅝ in) slices and arrange on a baking tray.

When ready to serve, grill the bread slices, turning once, until golden on both sides. Remove from the oven and, while still hot, firmly rub one side of each slice with the exposed flesh of half a garlic clove to infuse it with delicious garlic flavour.

Top each garlic-rubbed toast with roasted tomatoes, then a drizzle of the tomato cooking juices. Top with your choice of cheese or avocado and a little Basil Oil. Season with cracked pepper (you probably won't need salt). Serve immediately while it's still all warm, and before it goes soggy.

TIPS & SWAPS

- If you don't have time to make the Basil Oil, just use torn basil leaves instead.

# DUMPLINGS

**PREP** 1 hour, plus wrapping time

**COOK** 15 minutes

**MAKES** 35–40

Dumplings, dumplings, everyone loves dumplings! Making your own can take a little time as you master the folding of the pastry, but it's something that feels good because a) it's kinda fun and a novelty and b) you know what's gone into them is 100 percent the good stuff. In this case, lots of lovely veges and a simple, yet mouthwatering, blend of aromatics. I'm using store-bought wrappers here because that's where I draw the line these days but if you're keen to go the full monty, there's a dumpling pastry recipe in *Everyday Delicious*.

2 tbsp cornflour

2 tbsp soy sauce or tamari

1 tsp–1 tbsp sriracha, to taste

1 tsp sesame oil

1 tsp rice wine vinegar

2 tbsp peanut oil or other neutral oil, for frying

350–400g (12–14 oz) mushrooms, finely chopped

300–350g (10½–12 oz) bok choy, white and green parts separated and finely chopped

2 carrots, grated

3 spring onions, finely sliced

4 cloves garlic, crushed

1 tbsp finely grated fresh ginger

1 tbsp vegetable or imitation chicken or beef stock powder

¼ cup finely chopped fresh coriander leaves and stalks

40 store-bought round dumpling wrappers

**TO SERVE**

chopped fresh chives (optional)

soy sauce

chilli oil

Combine the cornflour, soy sauce or tamari, sriracha, sesame oil and rice wine vinegar in a small bowl. Set aside.

Heat the neutral oil in a wok or large pan over a medium-high heat. Add the mushrooms, white bok choy stalks, carrots and spring onions. Cook over a medium heat for about 7 minutes, stirring often, until soft.

Add the garlic, ginger and green bok choy leaves and cook for another 2–3 minutes until fragrant. Stir in the stock powder.

Give the soy sauce mixture a stir and add it to the vegetables. Stir over a low heat for a minute or two until thickened. Stir in the coriander. Remove from the heat. Transfer to a bowl and allow to cool fully before assembling the dumplings.

When ready to assemble, cover the stack of dumpling wrappers with a damp paper towel and have a small bowl or mug of cold water on hand for sealing the dumplings.

Working with one wrapper at a time, place about 1 tsp mixture (if you're greedy with the filling you won't be able to seal them properly) in the middle of the wrapper, keeping the edges clean of mixture. Dip your finger in the water and run it around the edge of the wrapper. Lift the wrapper, fold it in half and press the edges together firmly to seal. You can make three or four small pleats in the sealed rim if you like. Be sure they are completely sealed or the filling will smush out everywhere when you cook them.

Lay the dumplings on a plate, not touching, and cover with a damp paper towel as you continue to wrap the rest of the mixture.

Now choose your cooking method — they can be pan-fried or poached, and either way you'll need to cook them in batches.

To pan-fry the dumplings, place 3 tbsp oil in a pan over a medium heat, arrange the dumplings in a single layer in the pan and fry the bases for about 30 seconds, or until lightly browned. Add ⅓ cup water to the pan and cover with a lid. Allow to steam for about 5 minutes, then remove the lid and cook off all the excess water.

To poach the dumplings, fill a saucepan with 5cm (2 in) water and add 1 tsp salt. Bring to the boil and add 1 tsp neutral oil. Carefully drop in the dumplings and poach for a couple of minutes until tender.

Serve garnished with chopped chives (if using) and accompanied by dipping bowls of soy sauce and/or chilli oil.

## TIPS & SWAPS

- To make a quick dipping sauce, combine ¼ cup soy sauce, 2 tbsp hot water, 2 tsp coconut sugar, 1 tsp rice wine vinegar, 1 tsp toasted sesame oil and 1 clove crushed garlic in a small bowl.

# SMOKY PEA SOUP

**PREP** 15 minutes
**COOK** 1 hour 20 minutes
**SERVES** 8

An ode to my late oma, Lenie van Hoppe — and a recipe very dear to my heart. Welcome to the plant-based version of the original that appeared in my first book, *At My Table*. It's probably the heartiest, most satisfying soup you'll ever make (it's also decidedly economical using dried split peas, lentils and simple veges — one batch goes a long way). The whole cooking process feels like a joy, from the smell of the onions sautéed in butter, to the sight of an alarmingly large pile of chopped celery towering on your benchtop (be assured, it will reduce down), to the smoky and soulful aromas wafting from the generously filled serving bowl. Dipped with hot crusty garlic bread or crunchy toast on a chilly winter's evening, this is soul food in its purest form.

- ⅓ cup plant-based butter (regular if preferred) or grapeseed or sunflower oil
- 2 onions, finely chopped
- 8 cups vegetable or imitation chicken stock
- 2 cups water, plus more if needed
- 500g (1 lb 2 oz) dried split green or yellow peas
- 1 cup split red lentils, rinsed
- 1 kūmara, peeled and grated
- 3 large carrots, grated
- 1 bunch celery, very finely chopped (including some of the leaves)
- 1 leek, very finely sliced (discard tough outer leaves)
- 1 tbsp Vegemite or Marmite
- 1 tbsp paprika (use smoked paprika if you don't have liquid smoke)
- 2 tsp vegetable or imitation chicken or beef stock powder
- 1 tsp mustard powder or 1 tbsp wholegrain mustard
- 1 tsp liquid smoke (optional but recommended; see page 226)
- ½ tsp fine black pepper
- 1 cup finely chopped curly parsley or ¾ cup finely chopped flat-leaf parsley

**TO SERVE**

hot buttered toast

Heat the butter or oil in a large soup pot over a medium-low heat. Add the onions and cook for 10 minutes, stirring occasionally, until golden and soft.

Add the liquid stock, water, dried peas, lentils and kūmara. Cover with a lid (leaving a small gap) and cook over a low heat for about 30 minutes, stirring frequently, until the peas are tender. Skim off any froth that comes to the surface.

Add all the remaining ingredients except the parsley. It may all only just fit in — don't worry, it will reduce down as it cooks! Stir carefully then cover with a lid (leaving a small gap) and simmer over a low heat, stirring often to prevent sticking and burning, for another 30–45 minutes, or until everything is very soft.

Stir in the parsley, reserving a little for garnish. Check the flavours and season to taste with more salt and pepper if you think it needs it.

Serve with toast and the reserved parsley.

# SLOW POTATO & CHICKPEA CURRY

**PREP** 25 minutes
**COOK** 1 hour 30 minutes
**SERVES** 6–8

Making this authentic Indian-style curry feels like a beautiful ritual. For me it's a tremendously satisfying process, and a gentle reminder that not everything these days needs to be done as quickly as possible. To start, you prepare what is essentially a rich, flavoursome curry paste using sautéed onions, aromatics, tomatoes and spices — did you know it's good for the soul to make curry paste from scratch? You can get the curry going in the morning and come back to it as you need to throughout the day, which is what I normally end up doing. It'll be happy enough sitting there for a few hours between its various stages. And the flavours definitely develop over time — this one loves a fridge staycation.

- ¼ cup neutral oil, such as grapeseed or sunflower
- 1 tbsp whole cumin seeds
- 1 tbsp whole coriander seeds
- 6 large cloves garlic, finely chopped
- 2 tbsp finely chopped or grated fresh ginger
- 2 large onions, cut into 1cm (½ in) dice
- 250g (9 oz) tomatoes, cut into 1cm (½ in) dice
- 2 tbsp mild curry powder
- 1½ tbsp ground turmeric
- 2 tsp ground coriander
- 1 tsp nigella or black cumin seeds (optional)
- ½ tsp fine black pepper
- 2¾ cups vegetable or imitation chicken stock
- 800g (1 lb 12 oz) potatoes, peeled and cut into 2–3cm (¾–1¼ in) dice
- 400g (14 oz) can chickpeas, drained
- 2 tsp vegetable or imitation chicken stock powder
- 1½ cups frozen peas
- ½ cup coconut cream (optional)
- 1 tbsp maple syrup, agave syrup or coconut sugar
- 1 tbsp lemon juice or apple cider vinegar
- 2 tsp garam masala
- ¼ cup finely chopped fresh coriander leaves and stalks

**TO SERVE (OPTIONAL)**

- fresh coriander
- pappadums, roti or naan
- cooked rice
- coconut yoghurt
- brinjal eggplant chutney or Coriander Chutney (see page 216)

Heat the oil in a large, deep pan or casserole dish (ideally with a lid) over a low heat. Add the cumin and coriander seeds and cook for a minute until just sizzling and fragrant (don't let them get dark) to infuse the oil. Remove the seeds from the pan and set aside in a small bowl.

Add the garlic and ginger to the fragrant oil in the pan and cook, stirring every now and then, for a couple of minutes — you want them just golden, so be careful they don't burn.

Add the onions and continue to cook, stirring often, for about 7 minutes. They don't have to be totally soft yet.

Stir in the tomatoes, cover with a lid (leaving a small gap) and simmer over a very low heat for 20–30 minutes, stirring occasionally to prevent sticking, until the onions and tomatoes are soft and the raw flavour has gone.

Add the curry powder, turmeric, ground coriander, nigella or black cumin seeds (if using) and pepper and stir for a minute.

Add ¾ cup of the liquid stock (you don't want the spices to stick), then increase the heat and simmer rapidly for a few minutes until most of the liquid has evaporated and you're left with a mush.

Add the potatoes, chickpeas and stock powder and the remaining liquid stock and bring to the boil. Reduce the heat to low, cover and simmer for about 25 minutes, or until the potatoes are just tender.

Add the peas and coconut cream (if using) and cook, uncovered, for about 5 minutes until the peas are just tender.

Stir in the maple or agave syrup or coconut sugar, lemon juice or vinegar, garam masala and fresh coriander. Check the flavours and add more salt if needed (I needed nearly 1 tsp but you may need less).

To serve, top with fresh coriander (plus a little extra lemon and seasoning if you like) and enjoy with your choice of pappadums, roti, naan, rice, coconut yoghurt and chutney.

### TIPS & SWAPS

- If fresh tomatoes aren't in season, use a 400g (14 oz) can of chopped tomatoes instead.
- I use the Kara brand of coconut cream that comes in a carton for this recipe.

# FALAFEL

**PREP** 20 minutes, plus 1+ hours resting time

**COOK** 25 minutes

**SERVES** 4 with a salad and bread

- 1½ tbsp whole cumin seeds
- 1 tbsp whole coriander seeds
- 1 onion, quartered
- 1 large clove garlic, crushed
- 2 x 400g (14 oz) cans chickpeas, drained (I prefer organic)
- 1 cup loosely packed chopped fresh parsley
- 1 cup loosely packed chopped fresh coriander
- 2 tsp salt
- ½ cup chickpea flour, plus extra if shallow-frying
- 2 tbsp cornflour
- 1 tsp baking powder
- 1 tsp ground turmeric
- 1 tsp fine black pepper
- extra virgin olive oil, for frying (must be extra virgin)

**TO SERVE (OPTIONAL)**

- toasted pita breads (see page 210)
- hummus
- tabbouleh (see page 132)
- pickled red onion (see tip)
- fresh mint or parsley

There's been talk that canned chickpeas aren't a great option for falafel because the canning process breaks down the structure of the peas so the falafel tend to fall apart when you cook them (sludge in a pan, rage in my veins). But soaking dried chickpeas (if you can even find them), while a nice process, takes considerably more time and premeditation than just grabbing a couple of cans from the pantry – so I persevered. Blessed chickpea flour to the rescue! These falafel are moist and light on the inside, golden-crispy on the outside and totally scrumptious.

Heat a small pan over a medium-high heat. Add the cumin and coriander seeds and shake the pan constantly for a couple of minutes until they become aromatic – don't let them burn! Grind them with a mortar and pestle, spice grinder or coffee grinder, or place them inside a folded sheet of baking paper and use a rolling pin to smush them up (they don't need to be finely ground). Set aside.

Place the onion and garlic in a food processor and pulse until you have a chunky mince – not a purée. Add the chickpeas, parsley, fresh coriander and salt, and pulse again until you have a slightly chunky mixture. You want small chunks of chickpeas and herbs visible – don't purée everything to a complete mush. Transfer to a bowl, cover and refrigerate for at least 1 hour or up to 12 hours.

When ready to cook, combine the crushed spices, chickpea flour, cornflour, baking powder, turmeric and pepper in a small bowl.

Stir the flour mixture into the chickpea mixture until just combined – don't over-mix it. Gently roll into walnut-sized balls.

Now choose your cooking method – they can be either deep-fried or shallow-fried.

To deep-fry, place about 7cm (2¾ in) oil in a small saucepan and heat to about 170°C (325°F) (see tip). Working in batches, carefully drop in the falafel balls, being careful not to overcrowd the oil. Cook for 2–4 minutes, or until a deep golden brown. Drain on paper towels or a wire rack sitting over paper towels. Keep warm in a 100°C (200°F) oven while you finish frying the rest.

To shallow-fry, roll the falafel balls in a bowl of chickpea flour, dust off the excess flour and flatten the falafel into puffy disc shapes (balls may fall apart while cooking). Heat 1–2cm (½–¾ in) oil in a pan over a medium-high heat. When hot, fry the falafel in batches – don't turn them over until golden brown and crispy. Turn to cook the other side, then drain on paper towels and keep warm in a 100°C (200°F) oven while you finish frying the rest.

Serve on toasted pita bread with your choice of hummus, tabbouleh, pickled red onion and/or fresh herbs.

### TIPS & SWAPS

- Use 1 tbsp ground cumin and 2 tsp ground coriander in place of whole spices.
- To see if the oil is ready without a thermometer, dip the handle of a wooden spoon into the oil. If you see lots of fizzy bubbles form around the wood, your oil is ready for frying.
- To quickly pickle red onion, slice it thinly and toss it in a bowl with a pinch of salt and a squeeze of lemon juice.
- To reheat leftover falafel, fry in a pan with a small amount of olive oil.

# MINCE & CHEESE PIE

**PREP** 1 hour 15 minutes, plus cooling time

**COOK** 45 minutes

**SERVES** 6

When creating this recipe I wanted something as close to a good old classic Kiwi M&C pie as possible — like, proper tuckshop-esque feels. Lentils simply wouldn't do as the default here (although there's an option to sub them in the tips). So I've chosen textured soy protein, which ends up being so close to the texture of cooked beef mince that no one would ever know it wasn't (see page 227 for more info on that). So that's a win. As for the cheese component, because plant-based cheese tends to disappear when it melts, I've created a 'cheese sauce' layer so you can really see it (and get stuck into it). For a gluten-free option you could try gluten-free pastry sheets — or just make it into a scrumptious cheesy cottage pie with a mashed-potato topping.

### FILLING

- ⅓ cup extra virgin olive oil
- 2 large onions, finely chopped
- 2 large carrots, peeled and finely chopped
- 2 stalks celery, finely chopped
- 6 cloves garlic, crushed or finely chopped
- 1½ tbsp finely chopped rosemary leaves
- 2 cups dried textured soy protein
- 4 cups vegetable or imitation chicken stock
- ⅓ cup tomato paste
- 2 tbsp cornflour mixed with ¼ cup water to make a slurry
- 1 tbsp Vegemite, Marmite or gluten-free miso paste
- 1 tbsp malt vinegar
- 1 tbsp paprika
- 2 tsp soy sauce or tamari
- 1 tsp mustard powder or 1 tbsp dijon mustard
- 1 tsp imitation beef or chicken stock powder
- 1 tsp salt
- ½ tsp fine black pepper

### SAUCE

- ⅓ cup flour (gluten-free if preferred)
- 2 cups plant-based milk
- ⅓ cup grapeseed or sunflower oil
- ¼ cup nutritional yeast flakes
- 1 cup grated plant-based cheese

### TO ASSEMBLE

- 3–4 sheets flaky puff pastry (plant-based if preferred)
- ¼ cup aquafaba (the liquid from canned chickpeas), plant-based milk or a beaten egg

To make the filling, place the oil in a large casserole dish or deep pan over a medium heat. Add the onions, carrots, celery, garlic and rosemary and cook, stirring often, for about 15 minutes until the veges are soft and turning golden.

Add the soy protein, along with the remaining filling ingredients. Cover and simmer on a low heat for about 30 minutes, stirring frequently so it doesn't stick.

Remove the lid, then continue to simmer over a medium-low heat for another 30 minutes or more until you have a thick sauce. Remove from the heat. I always find it better to cool the filling right down before baking it in the pie — you can even leave it overnight in the fridge if you need to.

To make the cheese sauce, make a slurry with the flour and ½ cup of the milk. Transfer to a medium saucepan, add all the remaining ingredients except the cheese, and place over a medium heat. Stir constantly with a whisk for 5–10 minutes or until thickened up. It will be thicker than a normal white sauce. Using a wooden spoon, stir in the cheese. Season to taste with salt and pepper and set aside.

When ready to cook the pie, preheat the oven to 190°C (375°F) fan bake and set a rack in the lower half of the oven.

Line one large pie tin or two smaller pie tins with pastry. Add the cooled mince filling, then smoodge the cheese sauce on top. Brush the pastry edges with water where they will join and cover with a pastry lid. If you like, cut nice little shapes for the top.

Brush the top of the pie with the aquafaba, milk or beaten egg, prick a couple of steam holes and bake in the lower half of the oven for about 45 minutes, or until the pastry is deep golden in colour. You can give it another coating halfway through cooking if you like for more colour.

### TIPS & SWAPS

- You can pulse the carrots, celery and garlic in a food processor instead of finely chopping them — just don't let them turn to mush. I always chop the onions by hand as they seem to caramelise better.
- If you can't find dried textured soy protein, you can use 3 x 400g (14 oz) cans brown lentils (drained and rinsed) and pulse 400g (14 oz) mushrooms in a food processor. Add both at the simmer stage.
- Many brands of store-bought puff pastry sheets are 'accidentally' dairy-free as they contain vegetable oils rather than butter — check the ingredients.
- I use half a Massel beef-style or chicken-style stock cube in place of the stock powder.

# TOSTADAS

**PREP** 15 minutes
**COOK** 20 minutes
**SERVES** 4

1 red onion, very finely sliced
lemon juice
300g (10½ oz) tomatoes or cherry tomatoes, chopped small
¼ cup chopped fresh coriander, plus extra for garnish
8–10 small 'real' corn tortillas
extra virgin olive oil or neutral oil
sour cream, cheese sauce or aïoli (plant-based if preferred)
5–6 lettuce leaves, finely shredded
2 large avocados, diced or mashed
grilled corn kernels (optional)
lemon or lime cheeks
chilli or chipotle sauce or sriracha (optional)

**TOPPING**

2 tbsp extra virgin olive oil or neutral oil
1 large onion, very finely sliced
2 cloves garlic, crushed
2 tsp paprika
2 tsp ground cumin
1 tsp ground coriander
2 x 400g (14 oz) cans pinto beans, drained and rinsed (see tip)
1 cup vegetable stock
1 tbsp tomato paste
2 tsp coconut sugar
1 tsp salt

Honestly, before researching for this book I don't think I'd ever eaten a tostada, much less cooked one. Now I understand how delectable and fun to eat they are, I sit back and ask myself, whyyy? They don't seem to be widely known in New Zealand, but perhaps this recipe will change all that. I mean let's face it, soft tacos have been getting the glory for years now – it's high time for the sassy, crispy-based cousin to have time in the limelight (lime – see what I did there?). You HAVE to try them. Look for the smaller, authentic tortillas in the Mexican section of your supermarket – they have wonderful flavour and texture. I've also seen pre-baked tostada shells around!

To make the bean topping, heat the oil in a pan over a medium-low heat. Add the onion and cook for about 7 minutes until soft. Add the garlic and cook for another minute. Add the paprika, cumin and ground coriander with a splash of water, and stir for another minute.

Add the pinto beans, stock, tomato paste, sugar and salt and simmer until most of the liquid has reduced. Mash the beans to a chunky paste – it won't look very glamorous, but it needs to stick to the tortilla base as well as hold the toppings in place. Set aside until needed – you may need to add a little more water and warm it up again just before serving.

When ready to serve, preheat the oven to 180°C (350°F) regular bake.

Place the red onion slices in a bowl with a large pinch of salt and 2 tsp lemon juice. Stir, then set aside until needed. Drain before use.

Combine the tomato and fresh coriander in a non-metallic bowl with a squeeze of lemon juice, salt and pepper, for your tomato salsa.

Arrange as many tortillas as will fit on a baking tray. Brush both sides lightly with oil and bake for 10–12 minutes, until they're only very slightly golden and mostly crispy – they will finish crisping up as they cool and should end up totally crispy like a corn chip.

To assemble, spread sour cream, cheese sauce or aioli on each toasted tortilla. Top with some of the bean topping, lettuce, avocado, tomato salsa, red onion and corn kernels (if using). Sprinkle with extra coriander, a squeeze of lemon or lime juice and a little extra salt and pepper. Serve with your favourite hot sauce if you like an extra kick.

The tortillas should be strong and crispy enough to lift with both hands without everything falling off. Crispy, juicy and delicious!

## TIPS & SWAPS

- If you can't find pinto beans, use one can of black beans and one can of cannellini beans.
- If you have limes, try adding a little zest to the finished tostadas for extra zing.

# LOVE-YOU POTATOES

**PREP** 1 hour 20 minutes
**COOK** 20 minutes
**SERVES** 4–5

- 6 medium-large agria potatoes
- extra virgin olive oil
- 1 large onion, finely sliced
- 4 cloves garlic, crushed
- 1 tsp fresh thyme leaves (optional)
- 2 cups finely chopped kale or spinach
- 1 cup finely chopped celery
- 1 cup corn kernels
- ¾ cup grated plant-based cheese
- ½ cup chopped fresh herbs (I use a mix of mint, parsley and dill)
- 2 spring onions or ½ red onion, very finely chopped
- 2 tsp wholegrain or dijon mustard
- 1 tsp salt
- ½ tsp fine black pepper
- ¼ tsp fine white pepper

**TO SERVE**

- plant-based sour cream or aïoli
- 1 cup chopped plant-based bacon, fried
- fresh herbs (I use thyme)
- sweet chilli sauce or hot sauce (optional)

This recipe is based on one my mum Annemieke created for me as I held a newborn Sage in my arms, lost in a hazy baby bubble with no hope of cooking a thing. She'd grown the spuds in her garden and baked up a massive tray of them (freestyling the recipe, as she often does). I so clearly remember the feeling of overwhelming gratitude and tears flooding my eyes as I took the first bite. Knowing (and tasting) the love and care that had gone into not only preparing them, but growing and tending to them, too. It was the most nourishing and grounding thing I could have possibly hoped to eat in that moment, and I mean that in a spiritual and emotional sense as well as physical. I hope you find them just as special. (In her recipe there were smushed chickpeas and no bacon, FYI.) Oh, and in this photo, I used my very own first-ever homegrown spuds!

Preheat the oven to 200°C (400°F) and line a baking tray with baking paper.

Wash and scrub the potatoes to remove any dirt if necessary. Dry them, then coat with olive oil and sprinkle with salt. Prick each one a few times with a fork. Arrange on the baking tray and bake for 45–60 minutes, depending on how big your potatoes are, until easily pierced with a fork.

While the potatoes are cooking, heat 3 tbsp oil in a pan, add the onion and sauté over a medium-low heat for 7 minutes until softened and turning golden. Add the garlic and thyme (if using) and cook for another minute.

Add the kale or spinach, celery and corn and cook for a few minutes until softened.

When the potatoes are cooked through, remove them from the oven and allow them to cool slightly. Reduce the oven temperature to 180°C (350°F) regular bake.

When the potatoes are cool enough to handle, slice off the tops lengthways. Using a spoon, carefully scoop out and reserve the flesh, leaving a wall of flesh to hold the structure of the potato together.

Add the potato flesh to the pan with the vegetable mixture. Add the cheese, herbs, spring onions or red onion, mustard, salt and peppers. Stir to combine and cook for a minute to warm through. Check the flavours and adjust the seasonings to taste.

Stuff the potatoes with the filling — really pack it in and pile it up high. You might end up with a tiny bit of filling left, but you can probably get it all on there. Place the stuffed potatoes back on the lined baking tray and bake for about 20 minutes, or until hot throughout.

Serve topped with a dollop of sour cream or aïoli and scattered with the plant-based bacon and herbs. A crack of extra pepper and a little chilli sauce always goes well, too!

## TIPS

- You can stuff the potatoes in advance, store them in a sealed container in the fridge overnight, and bake them for 20 minutes at 180°C (350°F) regular bake when needed.
- The corn can be freshly cut from the cob, defrosted from the freezer or taken from a can and rinsed.
- You can get very nice plant-based bacon these days that crisps up well in a pan.
- Another way to check whether your potatoes are done is to pierce one from the top with a small paring knife — it should go through easily and lift out without lifting the potato up with it.
- Serve with a fresh salad.

# WINTERY PUMPKIN SALAD

**PREP** 1 hour 15 minutes
**COOK** 30 minutes
**SERVES** 4

I always say that when I'm eating a hunk of gorgeously glowing sunset-orange pumpkin in the depths of winter, it feels like I'm eating the stored-up sunshine from all those long summer days it spent soaking up the rays in the pumpkin patch. I really do believe that's what is happening, and it's a very beautiful thing. So, although this is a warming and wintry dish, I'll call it a salad anyway as it reminds me of that season. It's been on such a heavy rotation in my kitchen all winter, I'm surprised I didn't turn into a gangly blonde jack-o'-lantern by spring – I ate that much pumpkin. This dish is divine. Please try it out when pumpkin is in season, full of flavour and colour.

**RICE SALAD**

- 1½ cups brown basmati rice or wild rice
- 1 tbsp vegetable stock powder
- 3 tbsp extra virgin olive oil
- 2 onions, finely chopped
- 200g (7 oz) kale, chopped (discard thick stems)
- ⅓ cup raisins or currants
- 2 tbsp whole coriander seeds, toasted
- 1 tbsp soy sauce or tamari
- 1 tbsp lemon juice

**PUMPKIN**

- 1.5kg (3 lb 5 oz) crown pumpkin or butternut squash
- 1 whole bulb garlic
- 3 tbsp extra virgin olive oil
- 1 tbsp maple syrup

**DRESSING**

- ⅓ cup finely chopped fresh coriander
- ⅓ cup hulled tahini
- ¼ cup lemon juice
- ¼ cup water
- 1 clove garlic, crushed
- 1½ tsp maple syrup
- 1 tsp salt
- ¼ tsp fine black pepper

**CANDIED NUTS**

- ¾ cup chopped walnuts
- 1 tbsp olive oil
- 3 tbsp maple syrup

To precook the rice, cook according to the packet directions, adding the stock powder to the cooking water. Drain and set aside.

To make the dressing, combine the ingredients in a bowl or jug. Set aside.

To make the candied nuts, toast the walnuts and oil in a small pan over a medium heat for a minute until lightly toasted. Add the maple syrup and cook for another minute, shaking the pan all the time, until sticky and golden. Season with a little salt and pepper and remove from the heat.

To roast the pumpkin, preheat the oven to 190°C (375°F) fan bake and line 1 or 2 roasting trays with baking paper. Cut the pumpkin into 3cm (1¼ in) slices and remove the seeds. Arrange on the prepared trays and add the garlic bulb. Drizzle with the oil and maple syrup and toss to coat. Season generously with salt and pepper and bake for about 30 minutes until tender and starting to caramelise. Remove from the oven and set aside.

Prepare the rice salad. Place the oil in a large casserole dish or pan over a medium-low heat. Add the onions and cook for about 7 minutes, stirring until softened.

Squeeze the roasted garlic out of its skins and into the pan with the onions. Cook for another minute.

Add the kale with a splash of water and cook for a few minutes until tender. Stir in the cooked rice, candied nuts, raisins or currants, coriander seeds, soy sauce or tamari and lemon juice. Check the flavours and season to taste with salt and pepper.

To serve, arrange the rice salad on plates or a platter, top with the pumpkin and drizzle with the dressing.

**TIPS & SWAPS**

- You can precook the rice and prepare the dressing and candied nuts in advance if you like.
- Use spinach in place of kale if preferred.
- To toast the coriander seeds, place them in a small dry pan and over a medium heat. Cook, shaking every now and then, for a couple of minutes or just until you can smell a fragrance from them. Don't let them darken.

# CRÊPELETTES

**PREP** 15 minutes
**COOK** 10 minutes
**SERVES** 3 for a lunch or light meal

**Is it a crêpe? Is it an omelette? To be honest, I think it's a bit of both. Or maybe it's neither? Anyway, it matters not; these crêpelettes are utterly delicious and the most perfect speedy meal when you just can't be bothered with a big cook. And they're completely egg-free, I might add — made with chickpea flour, naturally! You'll want to double this recipe for a family-sized meal, and even serve a quick salad on the side. If you're using plant-based cheese I recommend stirring it through the hot sautéed veges so it starts to melt right away. If you're using regular cheese, it doesn't matter so much; you can add it as you assemble them.**

### BATTER

1 cup chickpea flour
1 tbsp nutritional yeast flakes
½ tsp baking powder
½ tsp salt
pinch ground turmeric (optional, for colour)
1 cup water

### FILLING

extra virgin olive oil or plant-based butter
½ red onion, finely sliced
¾ cup button mushrooms, finely sliced
1 cup chopped spinach
½ cup cherry tomatoes, chopped
½ cup grated cheddar cheese (plant-based if preferred)
2 tbsp finely chopped fresh parsley
1 finely sliced spring onion or 1–2 tbsp chopped chives

### TO SERVE (OPTIONAL)

lemon juice
chilli sauce, sriracha or tomato relish
aïoli or mayo (plant-based if preferred)
sliced avocado

To make the batter, place the chickpea flour, yeast flakes, baking powder, salt and turmeric (if using) in a medium mixing bowl, add the water and whisk until smooth. Set aside.

To make the filling, heat 3 tbsp oil or butter in a medium non-stick pan over a medium heat. Add the onion and mushrooms and cook for a few minutes until soft. Add the spinach and tomatoes and cook until the spinach is wilted. Season with salt and pepper. Remove from the heat, transfer to a bowl then stir in the cheese and half the parsley and spring onion or chives. Set aside.

To cook the crêpelettes, rinse the pan and set over a medium-high heat. When hot, add 1 tbsp oil or butter. Pour in a third of the batter and immediately swoosh the pan around to stretch it out as thinly as you can (if it's too thick, the crêpelette will go stodgy and fall apart). Leave to cook for 2–3 minutes until golden brown on the bottom and nearly cooked through at the top. Flip to just cook the other side, then flip back over.

Arrange a third of the filling over half the crêpelette surface, then fold the other half over on top of the filling, press down and leave to cook for about 30 seconds.

Turn out onto a plate while you use the remaining batter and filling to make two more crêpelettes. If you want to serve them together, just arrange the cooked crêpelettes on a baking tray and keep them warm in an 80°C (175°F) oven.

Serve garnished with the remaining parsley and spring onion or chives and your choice of lemon juice, hot sauce, relish, aïoli, mayo and/or avocado — whatever floats your boat (the more the better, in my humble opinion!).

# GNOCCHI'N ON HEAVEN'S DOOR

**PREP** 1 hour 20 minutes
**COOK** 30 minutes
**SERVES** 4–5

800g (1 lb 12 oz) agria potatoes, skin on
extra virgin olive oil
1 tbsp ground flaxseed
3 tbsp cold water
2 tbsp nutritional yeast flakes
1 tsp salt
¼ tsp fine black or white pepper
1 cup flour or high-grade flour (see tips for gluten-free)
grated plant-based cheese of your choice
lemon zest and juice, to finish

**SAGE OIL**

½ cup extra virgin olive oil
20 sage leaves
7 cloves garlic, finely chopped

I'll wager there'll be eyes rolling at this recipe title – a few people (read: critics) out there aren't fans of my foodie puns. What's not to love, though? In this recipe I've come through for all the egg-and-gluten-free folk who are craving a plate of soft, pillowy gnocchi in their lives. But honestly, even if you're someone who eats all and sundry without a care, you're gonna love it. I've served it with a very simple garlic and sage oil because, for me, the gnocchi-making process is usually enough without labouring over a sauce, but as another option feel free to toss the pasta through your favourite tomato or cream-based pasta sauce. See my note for gluten-free eaters, and just use whatever kind of cheese you prefer to eat for the topping. Serve with a fresh salad on the side.

Preheat the oven to 190°C (375°F) fan bake.

Place the potatoes on a small roasting tray, drizzle with oil, sprinkle with salt, prick the skins a few times with a fork and bake for about 45 minutes, or until a fork pierces through easily.

Stir the flaxseed and water together in a mug or small bowl and set aside for 5–10 minutes to thicken. Stir again before use.

While the potatoes are cooking, make the sage oil. Place the oil in a small saucepan over a medium heat. When hot, add half the sage leaves and fry until they stop bubbling, then transfer with a slotted spoon to paper towels and sprinkle with salt. Repeat with the remaining leaves. Add the garlic to the oil and immediately remove the pan from the heat.

When the potatoes are done, remove them from the oven and set aside until cool enough to handle. Cut in half, scoop out the flesh and use a spatula to push it through a coarse sieve (or use a potato ricer if you have one, that's always my preference) so it's smooth with no lumps. I find mashing it makes it gluey and a little lumpy – but you can do that if it's the only option.

Mound the potato on a clean benchtop with a well in the middle. Add the flaxseed mixture, yeast flakes, salt and pepper and mix gently with your hands. Sprinkle half the flour over the potato mixture and gently press it into the potatoes.

Sprinkle over the other half of the flour. Combine gently with your hands until you have a soft ball of dough – don't knead it firmly or you'll make it chewy. Cut the dough into quarters.

Gently roll each quarter into a rope 1.5cm (⅝ in) thick on a lightly floured benchtop and then cut into 1.5cm (⅝ in) pieces. Sprinkle with a little more flour to stop the gnocchi sticking to the bench and each other.

Bring a large soup pot of salted water to the boil. Drop in half the gnocchi. Once they've risen to the surface and sat there for a minute or two, transfer them to a colander with a slotted spoon. Drizzle with olive oil and shake gently to prevent them sticking while you cook the rest.

Heat a little olive oil in a large pan over a medium-high heat. When it's hot, add half the gnocchi and fry until golden and crispy on both sides. Transfer to a plate while you cook the rest.

When the second batch is golden and crispy, turn off the heat and return the first batch to the pan. Season with a little salt and pepper. Add the garlicky oil and toss to coat. Serve topped with the cheese, crispy sage leaves, a sprinkle of lemon zest and a squeeze of lemon juice.

**TIPS & SWAPS**

- To make this recipe gluten-free, use ½ cup chickpea flour and ½ cup cornflour in place of the flour – plus an extra ¼ cup water in the dough.
- Agria or other floury potatoes are essential for making 'dry' mash. You'll need about 6 medium or 3 large potatoes, but for this recipe it's best to weigh them to be sure.
- The uncooked gnocchi pieces can be kept in an airtight container in the fridge overnight.
- Flaxseeds (aka linseeds) are available from most supermarkets.
- Use 1 lightly beaten free-range egg in place of the flaxseed mixture.
- My plant-based parmesan would be the perfect finishing touch for this dish. You'll find the recipe in *Supergood* or on my website.

# STAUNCH CORN FRITTERS

**PREP** 30 minutes
**COOK** 30 minutes
**SERVES** 6 with veges or a salad

Staunch, because of the hidden bulk! I love to make a meal from a fritter by adding a few extra goodies to the bowl. Chickpeas are our bashful little heroes here. They go undetected as a protein boost, while the liquid from their can (aquafaba) is whipped to add lightness. This recipe makes a heap of fritters, so there's a bit of time spent over a frying pan ... but they're awesome a couple of days afterwards in lunches or for breakfast, or just add a fresh green salad or veges on the side for a quick meal. If you have fresh basil, dill or chives on hand, finely chop them and add to the mixture for a fresh zing.

400g (14 oz) can chickpeas
400g (14 oz) can corn kernels, drained, or 1½ cups fresh corn kernels
4 spring onions or ½ large red onion, finely chopped
4 cloves garlic, crushed
½ cup chopped rocket or spinach
½ cup finely chopped fresh parsley
2 tbsp soy sauce or tamari
1 tbsp sriracha (for spicy) or sweet chilli sauce (milder)
zest of 1 lemon
1½ tbsp lemon juice, plus 1 tsp for adding to aquafaba
½ cup flour or gluten-free flour blend (see page 222)
½ cup chickpea flour
½ cup cornmeal flour
¼ cup nutritional yeast flakes
1 tbsp baking powder
1½ tsp salt
1 tsp fine black pepper
1 cup unsweetened soy milk or other plant-based milk
neutral oil, such as grapeseed or sunflower, for frying

**TO SERVE (OPTIONAL)**

avocado chunks
fried plant-based bacon
sour cream or aïoli (plant-based if preferred)
chilli sauce or sweet chilli sauce
fresh herbs

Drain the chickpeas, reserving the liquid (aquafaba) in a medium mixing bowl. Tip the chickpeas into a large mixing bowl and mash until mostly broken up.

Add the corn to the mashed chickpeas, along with the spring onions or red onion, garlic, rocket or spinach, parsley, soy sauce or tamari, sriracha or sweet chilli, lemon zest and 1½ tbsp lemon juice. Stir to combine.

Combine the flours, yeast flakes, baking powder, salt and pepper in another bowl.

Add the milk to the corn mixture and fold through. Add the flour mixture and stir to combine evenly.

When ready to cook, add 1 tsp lemon juice to the aquafaba and beat with a whisk, hand beater or electric beater until thick, white and fluffy. Add to the corn mixture and gently fold through.

Heat 2–3 tbsp oil in a large pan over a medium-high heat (or use 2 pans to speed it up). Dollop ⅓ cup measures of corn mixture into the oil and cook for about a minute until golden and crispy, then flip and fry until cooked through. Transfer to a plate and keep warm in a low oven (80°C / 175°F) while you cook the remaining fritters.

Serve topped with your choice of avocado, plant-based bacon, sour cream or aïoli, chilli sauce and/or herbs.

## TIPS & SWAPS

- If you can't find cornmeal flour, I've tried this recipe using ¾ cup each of chickpea flour and plain flour, and it's worked fine.

# GOLDEN SPINACH & FETA PIE

**PREP** 1 hour

**COOK** 45–55 minutes

**SERVES** 6 with a salad and bread

- extra virgin olive oil (you'll need a bit!)
- 300g (10½ oz) firm tofu
- 600g (1 lb 5 oz) spinach
- 3 onions or 1 onion and 1 leek, very finely sliced
- 6 cloves garlic, finely chopped
- 2–3 tbsp hot water
- 2 tsp vegetable or imitation chicken stock powder
- 1 tsp white (shiro) miso paste
- ¾ cup plant-based milk
- ¾ cup chickpea flour
- ⅓ cup nutritional yeast flakes
- zest of 2 lemons
- 3 tbsp lemon juice
- 2 tsp dried oregano
- 1 tsp salt
- 1 tsp fine black pepper
- ½ tsp ground nutmeg (optional)
- ½ cup plant-based feta, crumbled
- ½ cup finely chopped fresh parsley
- ¼ cup chopped fresh dill or 2 tsp dried dill
- ¼ cup finely chopped fresh mint (optional)

**TO ASSEMBLE**

- 10–12 sheets filo pastry
- extra virgin olive oil or melted plant-based butter
- 3 tbsp sesame seeds, for sprinkling

Isn't it a glorious-looking thing? I spent a lot of time perfecting this recipe — it's not so simple to re-create a spinach pie in the absence of cheese and eggs, but by hook or by crook, I got there. The puffs of crispy golden filo delight me every time and make for such a cheerful and inviting-looking dish. It's the perfect light dinner or tasty lunch to make when you're enjoying an abundance of spinach or silverbeet from your garden (or when you have a couple of bags of frozen spinach in the freezer!).

Preheat the oven to 180°C (350°F) fan bake and brush a 30cm (12 in) oven dish with a little olive oil.

Break the tofu into a chunky mince texture and press very firmly in a clean, dry tea towel to absorb the excess moisture.

Add 3 tbsp oil to a pan over a medium-high heat. Add the tofu and cook until golden brown on the bottom, then stir and continue to cook until mostly golden all over. Set aside in a bowl and season with salt and pepper.

Add a few centimetres of water to a large saucepan, cover and bring to the boil. Add the spinach (jam it in there if necessary), cover and cook for a minute or so until wilted. Drain in a colander and rinse under cold water. When cool enough to handle, squeeze out the excess liquid. Chop the spinach roughly, then pull apart with your fingers to loosen any dense chunks. Set aside.

Return the pan you used for the tofu to a medium-low heat and add ¼ cup oil. Add the onions and/or leek and cook, stirring, for about 10 minutes until soft and golden and starting to caramelise. Add the garlic and cook for another minute. Remove from the heat and allow to cool.

Combine the hot water, stock powder and miso in a small bowl or mug and stir to combine. Transfer to a medium-large mixing bowl and add the milk, chickpea flour, yeast flakes, lemon zest and juice, oregano, salt, pepper, nutmeg (if using) and 2 tbsp extra virgin olive oil. Whisk to combine.

Add the fried tofu, cooked spinach, onion mixture, feta and herbs and stir to combine.

To assemble the pie, lay a sheet of filo in the prepared dish, brush lightly all over with oil or butter, then repeat with another three sheets.

Pour in the filling. Sprinkle with a little salt and cracked pepper and then cover with four more layers of filo, oiling each one as before. At the end, scrunch up the sides into the dish. For maximum pizazz, scrunch up a few more oiled filo sheets and arrange them on top.

Brush with a little more olive oil, sprinkle with the sesame seeds and bake in the lower half of the oven for 45–55 minutes or until a deep golden brown all over.

### TIPS & SWAPS

- You'll need two 400g (14 oz) bags of fresh spinach to yield 600g (1 lb 5 oz) once the thick stems have been removed. It's fine to swap some or all of the spinach for silverbeet (be sure to discard the white stems before weighing it) but it will take a little longer to wilt. Alternatively, you can use 500g (1 lb 2 oz) of frozen spinach — just defrost it then squeeze out the water.
- Add a couple of finely chopped spring onions or some chopped fresh chives for extra zing.

# THAI PEANUT SATAY SKEWERS

**PREP** 20 minutes, plus marinating time
**COOK** 15 minutes
**SERVES** 4

2 x 300g (10½ oz) blocks firm tofu

peanut oil or other neutral oil, for brushing

**MARINADE**

3 tbsp peanut oil or other neutral oil

1 heaped tbsp mild Thai red curry paste

2 tbsp soy sauce or tamari

1 tbsp lemongrass paste or minced fresh lemongrass (optional)

4 cloves garlic, crushed

2 tsp finely grated fresh ginger

2 tsp ground cumin

1½ tsp salt

1 tsp fine black pepper

1 tsp ground turmeric

**SATAY SAUCE**

400g (14 oz) can full-fat coconut cream

¾ cup crunchy or smooth peanut butter

¼ cup coconut sugar or maple syrup

2 tbsp mild Thai red curry paste

1½ tbsp lemon or lime juice, plus extra for serving

1 tbsp soy sauce or tamari

1 tsp salt

**TO SERVE**

cooked brown or white rice

chopped fresh coriander

½ cup chopped roasted peanuts (optional)

lime juice

Always a family favourite, these satay skewers may just become your summer staple. The tofu (which I wanted to *not* seem like tofu by the end) gets the proper royal treatment here — firstly marinated in all the delicious aromatics to infuse it deeply, then baked to add texture and 'chew', and finally grilled for that traditional smoky dimension, before being slathered in a rich, creamy peanut satay sauce (which you've balanced to perfection with hot, salt, sweet and sour flavours). Phew! It sounds like a lot but I promise you it's not, rather just a series of steps you can plan out in advance and cook when you're ready to eat. Serve with an Asian slaw (see my website or *Eat*), chopped cucumber or a green salad.

Cut the tofu into 2cm (¾ in) cubes and press gently in a clean, dry tea towel to absorb the excess moisture, taking care not to break up the cubes.

To make the marinade, combine the ingredients in a large mixing bowl. Add the tofu and very gently toss to combine, taking care not to break up the cubes — I use my fingers for this. At this point you can cover and refrigerate it for 24 hours until needed if you like.

When ready to cook, preheat the oven to 180°C (350°F) regular bake and line a baking tray with baking paper. Put about 15 wooden skewers in water to soak (the thick ones work best).

Arrange the tofu on the prepared baking tray, scrape any remaining marinade over the top and bake for 30 minutes.

While the tofu is baking, make the satay sauce by placing all the ingredients in a medium saucepan over a medium-low heat and simmering for about 5 minutes until thickened. Reheat it when you're ready to serve — it may need thinning with water to a pouring sauce consistency. Adjust with extra soy sauce, sugar, pepper and lemon or lime juice (you probably won't need more salt) until the balance of salt, sweet, hot and sour is to your liking.

Once the baked tofu pieces have cooled enough to handle, thread them onto the soaked skewers. Preheat a barbecue hotplate or grill to a medium-low heat. Brush the tofu skewers and the hotplate or grill with a little oil. Barbecue the skewers for 5–10 minutes, turning to grill evenly.

Serve on a bed of rice, topped with plenty of satay sauce and a sprinkling of coriander and peanuts (if using). Finish with a squeeze of lime juice.

**TIPS & SWAPS**

- If you can only find regular tofu, just fry the cubes without the skewers as they may break apart.
- Add a finely chopped makrut (kaffir) lime leaf or the zest of a lime to the marinade if you have it.
- Tamari is a good substitute for soy sauce if you can't eat gluten.
- If you don't have a barbecue handy, heat a little oil in a large pan over a medium-high heat, add the tofu skewers (you may need to do them in batches) and cook until nicely golden brown on all sides. You can also grill them under a medium grill (don't take your eyes off them!), or if you have a gas hob you can swish them in and out of the flames to add a little charcoal flavour.
- If you use chicken instead of tofu, skip the baking step.

# RED LENTIL & CARROT CURRY

**PREP** 15 minutes
**COOK** 30 minutes
**SERVES** 4–5

This is a beautifully uncomplicated dish that, once the initial prep is done, comes together in not too much time at all. Because the texture is quite singular I usually prefer not to serve it with rice, but if rice is your thing, go for it! Instead I serve it with flatbreads and added garnishes on top. I can't recommend the brinjal chutney enough, but you could go all-out and add sprouts, chopped cucumber, halved cherry tomatoes or whatever feels right to you. The flavour of the curry improves after a day, too.

- 3 tbsp olive, grapeseed or sunflower oil
- 2 onions, thinly sliced
- 4 cloves garlic, crushed
- 1 tbsp finely grated fresh ginger
- 1 red chilli, deseeded and chopped finely (optional)
- 1 tbsp mild curry powder
- 2 tsp ground cumin
- 2 tsp ground coriander
- 2 tsp paprika
- 1 tsp whole cumin seeds
- ½ tsp ground cardamom
- 2 cups grated carrot
- 2 cups split red lentils, rinsed
- 4 cups vegetable or imitation chicken stock
- 1 cup water
- 2 tbsp tomato paste
- 2 tsp ground turmeric
- ½ cup coconut cream
- 3 tbsp lemon juice
- 1 tsp salt
- ½ tsp fine black pepper

**TO SERVE (OPTIONAL)**

- naan, roti or garlic bread
- Coriander Chutney (see page 216)
- unsweetened coconut yoghurt (or extra coconut cream)
- brinjal eggplant chutney
- chopped roasted peanuts or toasted coriander seeds
- chilli flakes
- chopped fresh coriander or parsley

Heat the oil in a large pan or casserole dish over a medium heat. Add the onions and cook, stirring frequently, for about 10 minutes until very soft and turning golden. Add the garlic, ginger and chilli (if using) and cook for another minute or two.

Add the spices and stir for a minute, adding a splash of water. It should go into a mushy paste.

Add the carrots and stir for another 2 minutes.

Add the lentils, stock, water, tomato paste and turmeric. Simmer uncovered over a medium-low heat for about 15 minutes, stirring often so the bottom doesn't catch and stick.

Stir in the coconut cream, lemon juice, salt and pepper and simmer for another 5–10 minutes. If at any stage you need to thin the curry down, just add a splash more water. Or if you'd like it thicker, keep simmering. Check the flavours and adjust the salt, pepper and lemon until it tastes good to you.

Serve the curry hot in bowls, with whatever goodies you choose. It will keep in an airtight container in the fridge for a few days, or in the freezer for a few months.

# CHEESY GRILLED BURRITOS

**PREP** 40 minutes
**COOK** 45 minutes
**SERVES** 3–4 (makes 6 burritos)

So good it might just knock *Supergood*'s beloved Macho Nachos from their top spot on the podium, this is Tex Mex unapologetically jammed with flavour, designed to be devoured greedily by the whole family (even the staunch carnivores). It's reasonably cheap 'n' cheerful, easy and utterly satisfying to eat. Plus, you can prep the burritos in advance and cook them as you need them, which is a godsend (one I appreciate so much more now I'm a mum obeying little people's schedules and not my own). I find wraps easier to use than tortillas as they're big and pliable, and you're less likely to make a hash of it when you roll them up. It's not difficult, though, and after a few goes you'll have it down pat.

**FILLING**

extra virgin olive oil
1 large onion, finely chopped
1 red capsicum, finely diced
3 cloves garlic, crushed
400g (14 oz) can black beans, drained and rinsed
400g (14 oz) can corn kernels, drained and rinsed
400g (14 oz) can chopped tomatoes in juice
2 tsp vegetable or imitation chicken or beef stock powder
2 tsp mild smoked paprika
2 tsp coconut sugar
1 tsp ground cumin
1 tsp ground coriander
½ tsp fine black pepper

**TO ASSEMBLE**

6 large wraps or tortillas
1½ cups grated cheese (plant-based if preferred), or more to taste
2 cups cooked brown or white rice
chopped fresh coriander, plus extra for garnish
⅓ cup chopped red onion or jalapeños (optional)
lime zest and juice (optional)

**TO SERVE**

sour cream or aïoli (plant-based if preferred)
chipotle or chilli sauce

To make the filling, heat ¼ cup oil in a large casserole dish or deep pan over a medium-low heat. Add the onion and capsicum and cook, stirring frequently, for about 7 minutes until softened. Add the garlic and cook for another couple of minutes.

Add the remaining filling ingredients and stir to combine. Simmer over a medium-low heat for about 20 minutes, stirring every now and then so the bottom doesn't stick. Check the flavours and adjust the seasonings to your liking (you'll probably need at least ½ tsp salt). Allow to cool a little. At this point you can keep it in a sealed container in the fridge for a couple of days and reheat it before using. You want it to be quite warm, almost hot, before assembling.

When ready to assemble, preheat the oven to 160°C (315°F) and line a baking tray with baking paper.

If you're using wraps, there's no need to heat them first as they are usually pretty pliable. If using tortillas, warm them first to help them stretch – either splash with a little water and heat each side in a hot pan for 20 seconds, or microwave for 20 seconds.

Lay a wrap or tortilla on a clean benchtop and arrange about a sixth of the grated cheese in the middle, making sure there is about 5cm (2 in) of space each side so you can fold the sides in as you roll. Add about a sixth of the bean mixture, then rice, then coriander and a little more cheese if you like. Sprinkle with red onion or jalapeños and lime zest and juice (if using). Season with a little salt and pepper.

Roll up firmly, folding in the sides as you go so the filling is all contained and the edges are nicely tucked in and secure by the time you finish. Place seam-side down on the prepared tray while you roll the rest.

Heat a large pan over a medium heat (no oil). Add as many rolls as will comfortably fit, seam-side down, and cook until golden brown. Turn to brown the other side. Place back on the prepared tray while you repeat if necessary with any remaining rolls. Once all the rolls are browned, place in the oven for 10 minutes to heat through.

Serve garnished with a dollop of sour cream or aïoli, a drizzle of hot sauce and extra coriander.

TIPS & SWAPS

- Make sure you get large wraps or tortillas as small ones are a pain to roll.
- For my plant-based aïoli recipe see *Supergood* or my website. The Smoked Aïoli on page 220 would also work well here.

# FUSH PIE

**PREP** 1 hour 15 minutes
**COOK** 35 minutes
**SERVES** 6

'Fush' is Kiwi slang for fish, if you were wondering. Now, I was a tad worried that people would become alarmed at seeing banana blossoms in a fish pie and be put off making it. But I'd spent so much time perfecting it that leaving them out seemed a sad prospect. So I had a few people test it, and the consensus was that it was indeed wonderful. It's rich, comforting and smoky like a fish pie should be, without the fish (it's as close as you'll get, though) — all creamy and crunchy and bubbling and inviting and satisfying. The little stamens from the blossoms behave a bit like pseudo-fishbones and when you get the odd one and pick it out, it's quite the authentic experience (don't worry, they're soft). You'll want to read about magical liquid smoke on page 226 before embarking on this exciting journey. Serve with a fresh salad.

### FILLING

- 3 x 500g (1 lb 2 oz) cans banana blossoms in water or brine
- ¼ cup extra virgin olive oil
- ¼ cup plant-based butter
- 1 large onion, finely chopped
- 1 large leek, roughly chopped
- 2–3 large carrots, cut into 2cm (¾ in) pieces
- 2 stalks celery, cut into 1cm (½ in) pieces
- 5 cloves garlic, crushed
- ¼ cup flour or 3 tbsp gluten-free flour blend (see page 222)
- 2½ cups unsweetened plant-based milk
- 3 tbsp nutritional yeast flakes
- 1 tbsp dijon mustard
- 1 tbsp wholegrain mustard
- 1 tbsp grated horseradish
- 2 tsp dried dill or ¼ cup chopped fresh dill, plus extra for garnish (optional)
- 2 tsp vegetable stock powder
- 1 tsp natural liquid smoke (see page 226)
- 2 tsp salt
- ½ tsp fine white pepper
- 3 cups chopped spinach
- 1½ cups frozen peas
- zest of 1 lemon, plus extra for garnish (optional)
- 2–3 tbsp lemon juice
- 1½ tbsp maple syrup
- ⅓ cup chopped fresh parsley

### TOPPING

- 1.5kg (3 lb 5 oz) floury potatoes, peeled and halved
- ¼ cup plant-based butter
- 3 slices wholegrain or artisan bread, roughly chopped, or ¾ cup dried breadcrumbs
- extra virgin olive oil

To prepare the 'fish' for the filling, tip the banana blossoms into a colander and rinse well. Discard any large, loose outer leaves that feel tough and slippery. You want mostly the stems and stamens (the ugly bits). Take a few pieces in your hands and squeeze as hard as you can to get rid of as much liquid as possible. Loosen and shred into thin pieces with no big leafy chunks. It will no longer be a soggy-looking artichoke-type thing, but a shreddy, smoked-fish-esque fibre. Much better. Season generously with salt and pepper. Set aside.

To make the potato topping, simmer the potatoes in a large saucepan of salted water until just tender. Drain, mash roughly with the butter, season with salt and pepper and set aside.

While the potatoes are cooking, make the filling. Add the olive oil and spread or butter to a large pan or casserole dish over a medium heat. Add the onion, leek, carrots, celery and garlic with a pinch of salt and cook, stirring, for about 10 minutes until turning soft but not mushy.

Add the flour and stir for another minute or so. Add the milk and stir until thickened.

Add the yeast flakes, mustards, horseradish, dill, stock powder, liquid smoke, salt and pepper. Stir to combine, then add the spinach, peas, lemon zest and juice, maple syrup and parsley. Cover and cook over a medium-low heat until the spinach is wilted. Stir in the 'fish'. Check the seasoning and add more salt if needed and a crack of black pepper.

Pour the filling into a medium-large oven dish, then top with the potato topping. At this point you can cover it and leave it to sit for a few hours until you are ready to cook it, or refrigerate it overnight.

When ready to cook, preheat the oven to 200°C (400°F) fan bake.

Toss the bread chunks or crumbs in a bowl with a good splash of olive oil and season with salt. Scatter over the top of the potatoes. Bake uncovered for about 35 minutes.

Serve topped with extra dill and lemon zest if you like.

### TIPS & SWAPS

- If you have your own real smoked fish (caught sustainably), you can use 500g (1 lb 2 oz) flaked in place of the banana blossoms.
- If you want a flavour of the sea, finely chop 2 snack-sized seaweed sheets and toss through the 'fish' when seasoning it.

# ROASTED CAULI & KŪMARA LASAGNE

**PREP** 1 hour 30 minutes
**COOK** 1 hour
**SERVES** 8

- 1 medium cauliflower, cut into small florets
- 1kg (2 lb 4 oz) orange kūmara, peeled and cut into 3cm (1¼ in) chunks
- 1 whole bulb garlic (optional)
- ½ cup extra virgin olive oil
- 2 tbsp fresh thyme leaves

**TOMATO SAUCE**

- ¼ cup extra virgin olive oil
- 2 large onions, finely chopped
- 6 cloves garlic, crushed
- 1½ tbsp chopped rosemary leaves
- ⅓ cup tomato paste
- 3 x 400g (14 oz) cans chopped Italian tomatoes
- 1 cup water
- 2 tbsp coconut sugar
- 1 tbsp soy sauce or tamari
- 1 tbsp dried oregano
- 1 tbsp balsamic vinegar
- 2 tsp vegetable or imitation chicken or beef stock powder

**SPINACH**

- 300–400g (10½–14 oz) spinach
- zest and juice of 1 lemon

**WHITE SAUCE**

- 3½ cups unsweetened plant-based milk (I use soy milk)
- ½ cup plant-based butter or spread
- ½ cup flour or ⅓ cup gluten-free flour blend (see page 222)
- ¼ cup nutritional yeast flakes
- 1½ tsp salt

**TO ASSEMBLE**

- 400–500g (14 oz–1 lb 2 oz) dried lasagne sheets
- 10 fresh basil leaves, torn
- 1 cup grated plant-based cheese
- plant-based mozzarella (optional)
- fresh thyme sprigs

This lasagne is a thing of beauty. Every layer is seasoned and flavoured with tender loving care so when all baked and melded together, every mouthful is a beautiful, balanced and joyous experience. Instead of the usual pumpkin, I've used orange kūmara because here in New Zealand I reckon it's one of the best things we've got! Roasted up with thyme and garlic, it's pure heaven next to the earthy spinach, savoury cauli, creamy white sauce and rich, tangy tomato. The thing I love about this lasagne is it's versatile, so if you want to add a can of lentils to the tomato sauce, go for it. If mince is more your thing, brown it off and add that to the sauce instead. I invite you to make this recipe yours.

Preheat the oven to 190°C (375°F) fan bake. Place the cauliflower on one baking tray and the kūmara and garlic (if using) on another (or use one big tray if you have a wide oven). Drizzle each tray with half the oil. Season generously all over with salt and pepper, toss to coat and roast for 30 minutes, or until golden and tender, turning over once so one side doesn't get too browned.

To make the tomato sauce, heat the oil in a deep pan or casserole dish over a medium-low heat. Add the onions and cook for about 5 minutes until soft and turning golden. Add the garlic and rosemary and cook for another minute. Add the tomato paste and increase the heat to medium, stirring for a minute to caramelise slightly. Add the chopped tomatoes, water, sugar, soy sauce or tamari, oregano, vinegar and stock powder. Stir and simmer for about 20 minutes, or until reduced to a fairly thick sauce. Season to taste with salt and pepper.

To make the spinach layer, steam the spinach until tender. Drain, rinse under cold water then chop roughly. Place in a bowl, add the lemon zest and juice and season with salt and pepper. Toss gently then set aside.

To make the white sauce, place the ingredients in a medium saucepan and whisk to combine. Set over a medium heat and stir gently with a whisk for 5–10 minutes until it thickens up and turns glossy. Season to taste with pepper. If you need to thin it out with more milk later once it's been sitting a while, that's fine.

Once the roasted veges are done, remove them from the oven and reduce the oven temperature to 180°C (350°F) fan bake. If using garlic, squeeze it out of its skins into the kūmara. Add the thyme and roughly mash it all together.

When ready to assemble, grease a large, deep oven dish. Smear a spoonful or two of the tomato sauce on the base, then add a layer of lasagne sheets. Arrange the spinach mixture over the top, then add a third of the white sauce. Top with another layer of lasagne sheets, then the kūmara mixture and half the remaining tomato sauce. Add another layer of lasagne sheets, then the cauliflower and half the remaining white sauce. Add a final layer of lasagne sheets, then finish with torn basil leaves covered with the last of the tomato sauce and white sauce.

Top with the grated cheese, sliced mozzarella (if using) and extra thyme. Season with salt and pepper. Cover with foil and bake for 1 hour. Remove the foil and grill the top for a few minutes so it's bubbling. Remove from the oven and leave to sit for 15 minutes before serving.

## TIPS & SWAPS

- You can use butternut squash or crown pumpkin in place of orange kūmara.
- You can use 350g (12 oz) frozen spinach instead of the fresh spinach — just defrost it then squeeze out the water and chop.

# SUMMER RISOTTO

**PREP** 30 minutes, plus 4+ hours soaking time

**COOK** 30 minutes

**SERVES** 4

- 1¼ cups buckwheat groats
- 3 cups cold water
- 1 tsp apple cider vinegar
- 1¾ cups frozen peas
- 2 cups rocket
- ½ cup loosely packed (10g / ¼ oz) fresh mint leaves
- 1 tbsp lemon zest
- 1 tsp fine black pepper
- ½ tsp salt
- 3 tbsp extra virgin olive oil
- 1 onion, finely chopped
- ½ fennel bulb (200g / 7 oz), thinly sliced
- 1 zucchini, grated
- 4 cloves garlic, finely chopped
- ½ cup white wine (optional; see tip)
- 1 cup vegetable stock
- 2 tbsp white (shiro) miso paste mixed in ½ cup water
- 2 tbsp lemon juice
- 2 tbsp nutritional yeast flakes

**TO SERVE (OPTIONAL)**

- 2 zucchini or 1 bunch asparagus, chopped
- toasted pine nuts
- grated parmesan (plant-based if preferred)
- shredded lemon zest
- chopped fresh herbs
- extra virgin olive oil
- cracked pepper and/or chilli flakes

This isn't risotto as you know it — indeed, there's not a grain of rice in sight so technically it's not risotto at all, but who am I to split hairs? It's a fresh, summery, more healthful version that's oddly satisfying to make (that green herb purée, OMG) and a real delight to eat. The array of flavours is so remarkable that while you're enjoying it, I invite you to close your eyes and see where you drift off to. Sitting in a quaint restaurant somewhere in rural Italy, perhaps? Or a swanky cafe in Milan? To me, it's equal parts rustic and fancy-pants, and I love that so much!

Place the buckwheat in a bowl, add the water and vinegar and allow to soak overnight, or for at least 4 hours. If you've run out of time, place in a bowl, cover with just-boiled water and allow to sit for 15 minutes. Rinse well in a sieve or colander before using.

Bring a medium saucepan of water to the boil. Add the peas, cover and cook for 1 minute (it doesn't need to boil again). Drain in a colander and run under cold water until completely cool.

Transfer half the peas to a food processor and add the rocket, mint, lemon zest, pepper and salt. Whizz until smooth — you'll need to scrape down the sides a few times to get it going. Add the remaining peas and pulse a few times until you have a chunky texture with some big pea pieces. Transfer to a mixing bowl.

Place the oil in a large pan or casserole dish over a medium heat. Add the onion and fennel and cook, stirring, for a few minutes until the onion is translucent. Add the grated zucchini and the garlic and cook for another minute or so until fragrant, stirring all the time.

Add the drained buckwheat and cook for another minute. If using wine, add it to the pan and cook for a few minutes until most of the liquid has reduced.

Stir in the stock and simmer, uncovered, for about 10 minutes over a medium heat. At this point, you can leave it sitting for a few hours until you need it (refrigerate the pea mixture though).

When ready to serve, fry the chopped zucchini or asparagus (if using) in olive oil over a medium-high heat until tender and golden. Season with salt and pepper and set aside.

Stir the pea mixture and the miso mixture into the risotto. Simmer for a few minutes just to heat it all through. If you think it's too dry, add another splash of stock or water until it's a risotto-like consistency.

Stir in the lemon juice and yeast flakes. Check the flavours and season with salt and pepper only if it needs it — it may not as the stock and miso are salty already.

To serve, divide the risotto between bowls and top with the fried zucchini or asparagus and extra toppings of your choice.

### TIPS & SWAPS

- If you don't want to use wine you can replace it with ¼ cup red or white wine vinegar mixed with ¼ cup water.
- You could use basil leaves or spinach in place of rocket, but you won't get the peppery taste.
- You'll find my recipe for plant-based parmesan in *Supergood* or on my website.

# SPRING ROLLS

**PREP** 45 minutes
**COOK** 20 minutes
**SERVES** 4 for a snack or light meal (makes about 15 rolls)

- 2 tbsp peanut oil or other neutral oil, for frying
- 3 cloves garlic, finely chopped
- 2 carrots, julienned into thin strips
- 2 cups finely sliced cabbage
- 2 cups mung bean sprouts
- ½ cup walnuts, chopped
- 2 tbsp salt-reduced soy sauce or tamari
- 1 tsp maple syrup
- 1 tsp sriracha
- 1 tsp cornflour mixed with 1 tbsp water to make a slurry
- ½ tsp five-spice powder
- ½ tsp salt
- ½ tsp fine black pepper

**TEMPEH MINCE**

- 250g (9 oz) tempeh
- 3 tbsp peanut oil or other neutral oil, for frying
- 1 tbsp soy sauce or tamari
- 1 tbsp vegetable or imitation chicken stock powder (or 1 Massel cube dissolved in 1 tbsp hot water)

**DIPPING SAUCE (OPTIONAL)**

- ¼ cup soy sauce
- ¼ cup coconut sugar
- 3 tbsp water
- 2 tbsp lime or lemon juice, or to taste
- 2 tsp rice wine vinegar
- 1 clove garlic, crushed

**TO ASSEMBLE**

- 15 frozen square spring roll wrappers, defrosted
- 1 tbsp cornflour mixed with 2 tbsp water, for sealing
- neutral oil, for frying
- chilli oil, for serving (optional)

If you look up 'crowd-pleaser' in a dictionary, a photo of spring rolls might pop up and it'd totally make sense. I feel like it's well worth taking the time to put these crispy-shelled, moreish little flavour sensations together and wow the crowd with your apparently endless talents in the kitchen. Whether it's for nibbles with drinks at a gathering, a tray of party food that'll be quickly gobbled (even before the sausage rolls), or a simple dinner with a side slaw or salad, they're guaranteed to put a smile on everyone's face. I would double this recipe for a large family feed or a big nibbles platter.

To make the tempeh mince, break the tempeh into chunks and pulse in a food processor until you have a coarse crumb, a bit like mince.

Heat the oil in a wok over a high heat. Add the tempeh crumb and fry, stirring occasionally, for about 7 minutes until golden brown all over. Transfer to a bowl, then stir in the soy sauce or tamari and the stock powder. Set aside.

To make the filling, heat the oil in the wok you used to cook the tempeh. Add the garlic and fry for about 20 seconds. Add the carrots, cabbage and bean sprouts and stir-fry for about 5 minutes until everything has softened and reduced a little.

Stir in the tempeh, walnuts, soy sauce or tamari, maple syrup, sriracha, cornflour slurry, five-spice, salt and pepper. Remove from the heat and set aside to cool (you don't want to be wrapping the spring rolls with a hot mixture).

If making the dipping sauce, combine the ingredients in a small bowl and set aside until needed.

When ready to roll, cover the stack of wrappers with a damp paper towel or tea towel. Have the cornflour slurry ready. Line a tray with baking paper.

Carefully peel off one wrapper and lay it on a clean benchtop so it looks like a diamond with one point close to you. One side of the wrapper will be a little rougher to the touch than the other side — I like having the rough-side down.

Arrange a slightly heaped ¼ cup of filling in the bottom half of the diamond and begin to roll it up firmly, a bit like you would roll sushi. At about halfway, fold in the sides, then tuck them in as you continue to roll.

Moisten the top pastry triangle with the cornflour slurry and finish rolling up. Place on the prepared tray while you repeat with the remaining mixture. If not cooking immediately, you can cover and refrigerate them for a day or two, or freeze them until needed (make sure they aren't touching).

To cook, heat 5cm (2 in) oil in a medium saucepan over a medium-high heat. Wait until the handle of a wooden spoon bubbles rapidly when dipped in the oil before frying the rolls (if you have a thermometer, the temperature should be about 180°C (350°F)).

Using tongs, very carefully lower a few rolls into the oil and cook for a few minutes until golden all over. Transfer to a wire rack sitting over paper towels while you repeat with the remaining rolls.

Serve hot or warm with dipping sauce or chilli oil.

**TIPS & SWAPS**

- If you need to reheat the spring rolls later, either fry them in a dry pan over a medium heat, or bake at 160°C (315°F) for about 15 minutes.

# VEG-OUT MACARONI CHEESE

**PREP** 45 minutes
**COOK** 35 minutes
**SERVES** 6

- 500g (1 lb 2 oz) macaroni (gluten-free if preferred)
- 3 cups chopped spinach
- 2½ cups frozen peas
- ¼ cup finely chopped fresh chives or parsley, plus extra for garnish
- 2 cups (250g / 9 oz) grated plant-based cheddar cheese

### SAUCE

- 3 waxy potatoes, peeled
- 3 carrots, peeled
- 2 onions, peeled
- 2 cloves garlic, peeled
- 2 cups unsweetened plant-based milk (I use soy milk)
- ½ cup nutritional yeast flakes
- ⅓ cup hemp seeds
- ⅓ cup plant-based cream
- 2 tbsp neutral oil, such as grapeseed, sunflower or refined coconut oil
- 2 tsp white (shiro) miso paste
- 2 tsp vegetable or imitation chicken stock powder
- 1½ tsp dijon or wholegrain mustard
- 1½ tsp salt
- ¼ tsp fine white pepper
- ¼ tsp fine black pepper
- 8–10 fresh basil leaves

### TOPPING

- 1½ cups dried breadcrumbs
- 1 medium or ½ large onion, very finely sliced
- 2 tbsp extra virgin olive oil, plus extra for drizzling

Yes, there was a macaroni cheese in my last book, but I had a burning desire to create one that was considerably more nourishing so I could serve it up to my boys (and myself) knowing it was doing good. Basically, I've added lots of hidden veges, which is never a bad thing. The sauce is so simple, and it's kind of fascinating how the blended potato and veges thicken it up and render it 'cheese-like' in colour and texture. (Of course, you can sub in regular cheese here if that's what you prefer.) The flavour, however, comes from all the other added goodies (a little wizardry on my part) and the result is pretty dang delicious. Seconds all round?

Preheat the oven to 180°C (350°F) fan bake.

Cook the pasta according to the packet directions until al dente. Drain, then return to the saucepan.

To make the sauce, chop the potatoes and carrots, with the carrots being a third of the size of the potatoes so they cook evenly. Quarter the onions. Bring a large pot of salted water to the boil, add the potatoes, carrots, onions and garlic and simmer until tender but not mushy.

Drain the cooked veges and transfer to a blender or food processor along with the milk, yeast flakes, hemp seeds, cream, oil, miso, stock powder, mustard, salt, peppers and basil. Purée until silky smooth, then pour into the saucepan with the pasta.

Add the spinach, peas, herbs and half the cheese and stir to combine.

Tip into an oven dish and smooth out. Top with the remaining cheese.

To make the crumb topping, toss the breadcrumbs, sliced onion and olive oil in a bowl. Scatter on top of the cheese and top with a sprinkle of salt, a crack of black pepper and a small splash of olive oil.

Bake, uncovered, for 35 minutes until golden brown all over and bubbling. Scatter with chives or parsley before serving if you like.

### TIPS & SWAPS

- You can make this up to 24 hours in advance and refrigerate it, covered, until ready to cook.
- If your crew enjoys frozen mixed veges, you can use them instead of all peas. You could also add small pieces of steamed broccoli or cauliflower.
- I use a Massel chicken-style stock cube – one cube is the same as 2 tsp stock powder.
- Serve with a fresh green salad tossed with a sharp lemony dressing.
- Refined coconut oil is a flavourless oil that's able to tolerate high heat. It might be labelled 'coconut cooking oil' at the supermarket.

# SHEPHERD'S PIE

**PREP** 1 hour
**COOK** 35 minutes
**SERVES** 6

**FILLING**

¾ cup puy-style green lentils
⅓ cup extra virgin olive oil
2 onions, finely chopped
2 large carrots, peeled and finely chopped or grated
2 stalks celery, finely chopped
5 cloves garlic, crushed or finely chopped
2 x 400g (14 oz) cans brown lentils, drained and rinsed
2 cups vegetable or imitation chicken stock
⅓ cup tomato paste
1 tbsp white (shiro) miso paste
1 tbsp soy sauce or tamari
1 tbsp Vegemite or Marmite
2 tsp vegetable or imitation chicken or beef stock powder
2 tsp paprika
1 tsp salt
½ tsp fine black pepper
1½ tbsp finely chopped rosemary leaves

**MASH**

1kg (2 lb 4 oz) agria potatoes, peeled and chopped
500g (1 lb 2 oz) yellow or orange kūmara, peeled and chopped
¼ cup plant-based butter
¼ cup chopped fresh parsley or chives

**TO ASSEMBLE**

2 tbsp roughly chopped fresh mint
½ cup breadcrumbs
extra virgin olive oil

Oh so hearty, satisfying and bursting with all the delicious flavours of a traditional lamb version (the fresh pop of mint will make you feel lovely things), this is a doozie of a recipe for kids because it cleverly hides away loads of veges without any obvious offensively healthy protrusions. See if you can get away with adding finely chopped kale or spinach to the simmering mixture for even more green goodness. If you like, you can pulse the veges in a food processor instead of finely chopping them — although I always chop the onions by hand as they seem to caramelise better this way.

To make the filling, rinse the green lentils for 20 seconds under cold running water. Place in a saucepan with 4 cups of water and bring to the boil. Immediately turn the heat to low and cover with a lid. Simmer very gently over a low heat for about 20 minutes, or until the lentils are tender but still slightly firm in the centre. Drain and set aside.

Place the oil in a large casserole dish or deep pan over a medium heat. Add the onions, carrots and celery and cook, stirring frequently, for about 15 minutes until soft and starting to caramelise. Add the garlic and cook a couple more minutes.

Stir in the green and brown lentils, liquid stock, tomato paste, miso, soy sauce or tamari, Vegemite or Marmite, stock powder, paprika, salt, pepper and rosemary. Simmer over a medium-low heat for about 30 minutes until it has thickened into a nice sauce ready for the pie. Turn off the heat and set aside until needed — overnight covered in the fridge is fine.

To make the mash, simmer the potatoes and kūmara gently in salted water until tender (a fork will piece through easily). Drain well, then return to the saucepan with the butter, a big pinch of salt and a crack of black pepper. Mash roughly, adjust the seasonings to taste, and stir in the parsley or chives. Set aside.

Preheat the oven to 200°C (400°F) fan bake.

To assemble, pour the filling into a 30cm (12 in) oven dish or divide between six individual dishes. Sprinkle the mint on top of the filling, then add the mash in an even layer. Toss the breadcrumbs with a splash of olive oil. Scatter over the top of the pie and season again with a little salt and pepper.

Bake uncovered for 30–35 minutes, or until bubbling and golden brown.

**TIPS & SWAPS**

- You can make this in advance and refrigerate it, covered, for a few hours until needed.

# CREAMY MUSHROOMS ON TOAST

**PREP** 15 minutes
**COOK** 25 minutes
**SERVES** 2

- 2 tbsp oil or plant-based butter
- ½ onion, finely chopped
- 3 cloves garlic, crushed or finely chopped
- 400g (14 oz) brown button mushrooms, cut into 5mm (¼ in) slices
- 300g (10½ oz) portobello mushrooms, cut into 5mm (¼ in) slices
- ½ cup vegetable stock
- 1 tbsp lemon juice
- 1 cup cream, soy cream or other plant-based cream
- 1 tsp wholegrain or dijon mustard
- 2 tsp fresh thyme leaves (optional)
- ¼ cup finely chopped fresh parsley and/or chives

**TO SERVE**

- hot buttered toast
- finely chopped fresh parsley and/or thyme leaves

There's something undeniably satisfying about mushrooms on toast — it's a deliciously simple, quick-as-a-flash meal for any occasion, be it breakfast, brunch, lunch or dinner. And if you're like me, sometimes it's the only thing you feel like and nothing else will do. Google says there are more than 2000 varieties of edible mushrooms in the world — I've suggested using two here (baby steps) because there's such an impressive variety available in supermarkets now and it's fun to explore their different textures and flavours. This recipe serves two, so double it for a larger meal.

Heat the oil or butter in a large pan over a medium-low heat. Add the onion and fry for about 7 minutes until soft and fragrant. Add the garlic and cook for another minute.

Stir in the mushrooms and increase the heat to medium-high. Cook for about 5 minutes until the mushrooms are tender and most of the liquid has evaporated.

Add the stock and lemon juice and simmer rapidly until the liquid has almost disappeared.

Add the cream, mustard and thyme (if using), and simmer rapidly again until it's the right consistency to pour over toast.

Stir in the parsley and/or chives. Check the flavours and season to taste with salt and pepper.

Serve on buttered toast, topped with parsley and/or thyme.

### TIPS & SWAPS

- If you can't find dairy-free cream (it's usually in a carton called soy cream or plant-based cream at the supermarket), you can use a blender or bullet to whizz up ⅓ cup neutral oil and ⅔ cup unsweetened soy milk instead. Or use regular cream.
- If you see enoki mushrooms at your local, buy some and sauté them in butter for a few minutes to finish the dish off.

# SAUSAGE PASTA BAKE

**PREP** 40 minutes
**COOK** 25 minutes
**SERVES** 4–5

The thing I love about this dish is that it provides many of the comforting, familiar pleasures of a lasagne with far less effort (and fewer dishes). We could think of it as the rip shit 'n' bust version (I could probably come up with a more appetising name than that, though). It's also a convenient dish that's happy being prepared in advance – later on you simply bake it, swing it bubbling from the oven and present it to a sea of hungry faces with an air of accomplished victory. Served with a crisp green salad with a balsamic dressing, it's hearty, family-style food that'll have them coming back for more.

300g (10½ oz) dried pasta (shells or penne work well)
500–600g (1 lb 2 oz–1 lb 5 oz) good-quality sausages (plant-based if preferred)
extra virgin olive oil
2 onions, finely chopped
2–3 carrots, peeled and grated
1–2 zucchini, grated
5 cloves garlic, crushed
2 tsp dried oregano, plus extra for sprinkling
600–680g (1 lb 5 oz–1 lb 8 oz) passata
400g (14 oz) can brown lentils, drained and rinsed
¾ cup water
¼ cup tomato paste
3 tbsp coconut sugar or 2 tbsp maple syrup
2 tbsp vegetable or imitation beef or chicken stock powder
1 tbsp paprika
1 tbsp balsamic vinegar
2 tsp soy sauce or tamari
1 tsp salt
¼ tsp fine black pepper
½ cup roughly chopped mixed pitted deli olives (optional)
torn fresh basil leaves, plus extra for garnish

**WHITE SAUCE**

⅓ cup plant-based butter
¼ cup flour or gluten-free flour blend (see page 222)
1¾ cups unsweetened soy milk or other plant-based milk
¼ cup nutritional yeast flakes
1 tsp salt
¼ tsp fine white pepper

**TO ASSEMBLE**

1½ cups grated cheddar cheese (plant-based if preferred)
1–2 tbsp fresh thyme leaves
extra virgin olive oil

Preheat the oven to 190°C (375°F) fan bake and have a large oven dish ready (one you'd use for lasagne).

Cook the pasta according to the packet directions. Drain in a colander and toss with a little olive oil.

Place the sausages in a cold casserole dish or deep pan with a little oil. Cook over a medium-high heat until the sausages are cooked through and browned all over. Set aside to cool, then cut into 5mm (¼ in) slices. Drain away any excess fat from the pan (I like to keep 1–2 tsp for cooking the onions).

Add another ¼ cup oil to the pan, along with the onions, carrots and zucchini and cook over a medium heat, stirring occasionally, for about 7 minutes until soft and fragrant. Add the garlic and oregano and cook for another few minutes.

Add the passata, lentils, water, tomato paste, coconut sugar or maple syrup, stock powder, paprika, vinegar, soy sauce or tamari, salt and pepper to the pan and simmer over a medium heat for about 10 minutes until reduced down to a thickish sauce – but still with some moisture remaining so the bake isn't dry. Stir in the sliced sausages and the olives (if using).

To make the white sauce, heat the butter and flour in a small saucepan over a medium-low heat, stirring for a few minutes until puffy. Remove from the heat and slowly pour in the milk while stirring with a whisk to avoid lumps. Stir in the yeast flakes, salt and pepper. Return to a medium heat and stir constantly with a whisk until thickened – it will happen all of a sudden. If it seems too thick you can thin it down with extra milk. Set aside.

To assemble, stir the pasta and basil leaves through the tomato sauce and transfer it to the oven dish. Pour the white sauce over the top and scatter with the cheese and thyme. Give it another crack of pepper and a little extra dried oregano if you like. Add another drizzle of oil to help it brown up.

Cover with foil and bake for 25–30 minutes until hot. If you like, you can remove the foil and place it under the grill to brown the top and finish melting the cheese. Serve topped with basil.

## TIPS

- If you can be bothered, toss breadcrumbs or torn bread in olive oil and scatter on top before baking.
- If using regular sausages, look for those without added preservatives or other nasties.
- For a different texture, try squeezing the sausage meat out of the casings and frying it up like mince before you add it to the sauce.

# SUSHI BOWLS

**PREP** 1 hour
**SERVES** 4

- 1 large telegraph cucumber
- 4 cups cooked white, brown or wild rice
- 1–2 avocados, sliced or diced
- julienned carrot and/or finely chopped crispy lettuce
- extra soy sauce (stir in a little wasabi if desired)
- chopped spring onion or chives
- ⅓ cup toasted sesame seeds
- 1–2 sheets nori (sushi seaweed), thinly sliced
- pickled sushi ginger (optional)

**DRESSING**

- ⅔ cup hulled tahini
- ½ cup water, plus more if needed
- 2–3 tbsp lemon juice, or to taste
- 1 clove garlic, crushed
- 2 tsp white (shiro) miso paste
- 2 tsp toasted sesame oil
- 2 tsp ginger juice (squeeze finely grated fresh ginger)
- 2 tsp soy sauce or tamari
- 1½ tsp salt

**TEMPEH**

- 3 tbsp peanut oil or other neutral oil
- 600g (1 lb 5 oz) tempeh, cut into thin strips
- ¼ cup soy sauce or tamari
- 1 stock cube of your choice (I use Massel), dissolved in 2 tbsp boiled water

The flavours of sushi are something I absolutely delight in, but the process of rolling homemade sushi is something I don't quite have the patience for these days (with two boys under five at the time of writing — enough said). Using this recipe you can prep it all up in advance, fry the lovely crispy tempeh last then freestyle it all into bowls when you're ready to eat. You still get that inimitable sushi vibe with the rice, nori, wasabi, soy sauce and even pickled ginger if you want it. The tahini dressing adds a welcome creamy dimension we didn't know we needed, but we do. Feel free to mix it up and use whatever protein you'd normally select in your sushi tray.

To make the dressing, whisk the ingredients in a small jug or bowl and set aside. If it's too thick to drizzle you can thin it down with a little water before serving.

To prepare the tempeh, heat the oil in a large pan over a medium heat. Add the tempeh slices and fry for about 6–7 minutes until crispy and deep golden on both sides. Set aside to cool a little.

Combine the soy sauce or tamari and stock mixture in a bowl. When the tempeh is cool enough to handle, dip it in the soy and stock mixture.

Cut the cucumber in half lengthways, scrape the seeds out with a teaspoon and discard them. Use a peeler to cut the flesh into long strips. If desired, place in a bowl, season with salt and pepper and a dash of rice wine vinegar if you have it, and set aside for 5 minutes.

To serve, divide the rice between serving bowls and top with the tempeh, cucumber, avocado and carrot and/or lettuce. Drizzle with soy sauce and season with cracked pepper. Finish with a generous drizzle of dressing and a sprinkle of spring onion or chives and sesame seeds. Let people scatter their own nori and pickled ginger (if using) over the top.

### TIPS & SWAPS

- You'll need 2 cups uncooked rice to yield 4 cups cooked rice.
- For colour and extra protein, add frozen edamame beans (young soy beans) that have been soaked in boiling water for 5 minutes.
- To toast the sesame seeds, dry-roast in a small pan for a few minutes, shaking occasionally, until golden and fragrant.
- If you have a gas hob, you can wave the nori quickly over the flames (not too close or it will burn) until it turns crispy and toasty, then crumble it into small pieces. If not, just fold it and snip it into small pieces with kitchen scissors.

# SIMPLE CAULIFLOWER RICE

**PREP** 20 minutes
**COOK** 40 minutes
**SERVES** 4

This is another one of those recipes I came up with while on summer holiday at Great Barrier, where there's always a limited selection of ingredients and I just have to make do — which is actually a nice challenge! This dish came together nicely, so nicely in fact that it's made it into this book with very few edits to the original. I guess I'm just in a super happy space and flow when I'm over there. All the simple components add up to something delicious and a bit of a change from the usual.

1 medium-large cauliflower, cut into 2–3cm (¾–1¼ in) chunks
neutral oil, such as grapeseed, sunflower or coconut
2–3 zucchini, cut into 2cm (¾ in) dice
2 onions, finely sliced
4 cloves garlic, crushed
1 tbsp mild curry powder
2 tsp paprika
2 tsp ground coriander
1 tsp whole cumin seeds
1 tsp ground turmeric
½ tsp chilli powder (optional)
2 tsp vegetable stock powder dissolved in ¼ cup hot water
⅓ cup raisins or currants
2 tbsp lemon juice
1 tbsp maple syrup

**RICE**
¾ cup basmati rice
2 tbsp vegetable stock powder

**TO SERVE**
chopped fresh parsley or coriander
unsweetened yoghurt or coconut yoghurt
brinjal eggplant chutney or Coriander Chutney (see page 216)

Cook the rice according to the packet directions, adding the stock powder to the cooking water. Drain and set aside.

Steam or simmer the cauliflower for a few minutes until it's half-cooked. Set aside.

Heat 2 tbsp oil in a very large, deep pan or casserole dish over a high heat, then sear the zucchini until golden but not mushy. Transfer to a bowl and set aside.

Add 3 tbsp oil to the same pan over a medium heat. Add the onions and cook, stirring occasionally, for about 10 minutes. Turn up the heat to medium-high and cook, stirring frequently, until it starts to turn a little golden and caramelised.

Add the garlic, curry powder, paprika, ground coriander, cumin seeds, turmeric and chilli powder (if using), along with the stock and water mixture, and stir for another minute or so.

Add the cauliflower to the pan and cook for another 5 minutes until tender.

Add the cooked rice and the raisins or currants and give it another stir.

Just before serving, stir in the cooked zucchini, lemon juice and maple syrup. Check the flavours and season to taste with salt and pepper.

Serve in bowls, scattered with parsley or coriander and accompanied by yoghurt and/or chutney for extra oomph and spice.

## TIPS & SWAPS

- Don't chop the cauliflower too finely, or it will turn to mush in the pan.

# CURRY PUFF SAUSAGE ROLLS

**PREP** 45 minutes
**COOK** 25–30 minutes
**SERVES** 5–6 for a meal with sides

I couldn't let this book sneak through to the printers without adding a sausage roll recipe. In *Supergood* I gave you a spin on a more traditional mushroomy lentil mince vibe; here I'm taking your taste buds on a journey through the aromatic layers of a fragrant Indian curry! With the pastry, it sort of reminds me of a curry puff (woohoo!). These work well served with the quintessential Kiwi ketchup, but if you want to be a little fancier and more on-point, try chutney or relish. You can use regular chutney or relish, or brinjal eggplant chutney mixed with coconut yoghurt if you like it spicier, or a little mango chutney for a sweeter finish.

- 650g (1 lb 7 oz) agria potatoes, peeled and cut into 2–3cm (¾–1¼ in) dice
- ¼ cup extra virgin olive oil
- 2 onions, finely chopped
- 5 cloves garlic, crushed or finely chopped
- 2 tbsp mild curry powder
- 2 tsp paprika
- 2 tsp ground coriander
- 1 tsp whole cumin seeds
- ¼ cup water
- ¼ cup good-quality fruit chutney
- ¾ cup frozen mixed vegetables
- 400g (14 oz) can chickpeas
- ⅓ cup finely chopped fresh coriander and/or parsley
- 1 tbsp vegetable or imitation chicken stock powder
- 1 tbsp coconut sugar
- 2 tsp lemon juice
- 2 tsp salt
- ¾ tsp fine black pepper

**TO ASSEMBLE**

- 4 sheets flaky puff pastry (plant-based if preferred), defrosted
- liquid from the chickpeas (aquafaba) or a beaten egg, for glazing
- fennel, poppy or sesame seeds (optional)

Steam or simmer the potatoes in salted water until tender. Drain and set aside.

Heat the oil in a pan over a medium-low heat. Add the onions and cook, stirring, for about 12 minutes until golden. Add the garlic and cook for another minute. Add the curry powder, paprika, ground coriander, cumin seeds and water and cook for another 30 seconds, stirring to a mush. Add the chutney and frozen veges and stir for another minute.

Drain the chickpeas, reserving the liquid (aquafaba) for brushing the pastry if you don't eat eggs. Tip the chickpeas into the pan, stir it up and then mash briefly so you have some whole chickpeas and some chunks. Add the cooked potatoes, herbs, stock powder, coconut sugar, lemon juice, salt and pepper. Give it all a good stir to rough the potatoes up a bit. Set aside to cool right down, or refrigerate until needed.

When ready to cook, preheat the oven to 200°C (400°F) fan bake and line a baking tray with baking paper.

To assemble, place a pastry sheet on a clean, dry benchtop. Cut in half across the middle so you have two horizontal rectangles. Working with one half at a time, arrange about an eighth of the filling in a neat log lengthways across the middle of the rectangle. Brush water on both long edges, then fold up both long edges to snugly meet on top. Press to seal. Repeat with the remaining pastry and filling.

Brush the rolls all over with the reserved aquafaba or beaten egg. You can leave them whole for a meal or use a serrated knife to cut them into short lengths for party food.

Place seam-side down a few centimetres apart on the prepared tray. Brush the tops with more aquafaba or beaten egg and prick with a fork. Sprinkle with seeds (if using).

Bake in the lower half of the oven for about 25 minutes until the pastry is golden brown and puffed up. Allow to cool a little before serving. You may need to squish the filling back in if it has puffed out the sides a bit.

## TIPS & SWAPS

- If you don't eat dairy, look for puff pastry made with vegetable oil or fat instead of butter.

# MUSHROOMY MISO NOODLE SOUP

**PREP** 35 minutes
**COOK** 10 minutes
**SERVES** 4

- 100g (3½ oz) fresh shiitake mushrooms, very finely sliced
- 100g (3½ oz) brown button mushrooms, very finely sliced
- 1 tbsp soy sauce or tamari
- 2 tsp toasted sesame oil
- 2 tsp finely grated fresh ginger
- 2 cloves garlic, crushed
- 500g (1 lb 2 oz) firm tofu, coarsely grated
- 3 tbsp peanut oil or other neutral oil, for frying
- 300g (10½ oz) dried soba or gluten-free noodles
- 6 cups vegetable or imitation chicken stock
- 2 cups water
- 1 tsp Vegemite or Marmite
- ¼ tsp fine black pepper
- 100g (3½ oz) chopped Asian greens, such as baby bok choy or pak choy
- 4 tbsp white (shiro) miso paste
- 3 spring onions, very finely sliced

**TO SERVE (OPTIONAL)**

- ¼ cup finely chopped chives
- toasted sesame seeds

There's that miso fella again, and he brought his mates to the party! I mean, looking at the ingredients here (I've gone to town with flavour's most-wanted list), you just know your mouth is in for a hefty savoury explosion with every slurp. Welcome to umami central: mushrooms, miso, tamari, Marmite (ha). I'd recommend not adding salt until the end because, depending on your stock, it may be seasoned enough already. I can guarantee a big steaming bowl of this with buttered toast will fill you with cheer on a chilly evening.

Place the sliced mushrooms in a bowl, add the soy sauce or tamari, sesame oil, ginger and garlic and toss to combine evenly. Set aside so the flavours can infuse.

Press the grated tofu in a clean, dry tea towel to absorb the excess moisture.

Heat the oil in a pan over a medium-high heat. When hot, add the tofu and fry for about 7 minutes until golden brown and crispy all over. Set aside on paper towels.

Cook the noodles according to the packet directions so they still have a little bite. Drain in a colander and rinse under cold water. Set aside.

Place the stock, water, Vegemite or Marmite and pepper in a large saucepan over a medium heat and bring to a simmer. Add the mushrooms and greens and simmer for about 5 minutes until the mushrooms are tender. Turn off the heat.

Place the miso in a small bowl. Add ½ cup of the hot broth and stir with a fork to combine. Add to the broth along with three-quarters of the spring onions, and stir to combine.

If not serving immediately, you can turn on the heat again briefly to heat the broth through, but don't let it boil once the miso is added (the aromatic qualities of miso — as well as some of the nutritional benefits — are damaged when boiled).

To serve, divide the noodles between bowls and ladle the broth over the top. Garnish with the fried tofu and reserved spring onions and a sprinkling of chives and sesame seeds (if using).

### TIPS & SWAPS

- If you can't find shiitake mushrooms, just use more button mushrooms. If you're lucky enough to get your hands on other exotic Asian mushrooms, such as enoki or oyster mushrooms, you can add the chopped oyster mushrooms in with the simmer, and the enoki at the end as a garnish.
- You can leave out the tofu if you prefer a simpler, lighter soup.
- Tamari is a good substitute for soy sauce if you can't eat gluten. Look for sodium-reduced soy sauce and tamari if possible.
- For an additional garnish, finely slice or crumble a sheet of nori (sushi seaweed). If you have a gas hob, you can wave the nori quickly over the flames (not too close or it will burn) until it turns crispy and toasty, then crumble it into small pieces. If not, just fold it and snip it into small pieces with kitchen scissors.

# BUBBLING POTATO BAKE

**PREP** 20 minutes
**COOK** 1 hour 15 minutes
**SERVES** 8

1.75–2kg (3 lb 13 oz–4 lb 8 oz) agria potatoes, peeled
1 large onion, peeled
400g (14 oz) can chickpeas, drained
2 cups unsweetened soy milk or other creamy plant-based milk
1 cup soy cream
½ cup nutritional yeast flakes
2 tsp vegetable or imitation chicken stock powder
2 tsp dijon mustard
1¼ tsp salt
¼ tsp white pepper
¾ cup grated plant-based cheese
2 tsp fresh thyme leaves (optional)
¾ cup dried breadcrumbs (or whizz up fresh bread)
extra virgin olive oil

Oh, how I love potatoes (you've probably got the hint now after leafing through this book). I especially love slicing them to smithereens, layering them into a luscious, bubbling baked showpiece interlaced with onions and topped with herbs and crunchy crumb. The genius here is that the chickpeas add a rich creaminess to the sauce; you'd never know they were there but they add a little protein kick so you can enjoy the bake either as a side dish or as the star of a meal, perhaps with a crisp green salad or tomato salad or steamed greens. A little garlic bread, too, if you please? My kids love to eat this, so I make it a lot. I'm sure yours will, too.

Preheat the oven to 180°C (350°F) fan bake and grease a large, deep oven dish with olive oil.

Using a mandolin if you have one, slice the potatoes and onion into 3mm (⅛ in) slices. If you don't have a mandolin, slice them by hand. It helps to cut a thin slice off one side, then use the cut side as a stable platform on the board while you slice.

Arrange a layer of potato slices in the base of the prepared dish, generously overlapping each other. Season with a little salt and cracked pepper. Follow with a little sliced onion. Continue this layering until all the potato is used up, finishing with a layer of onion on top if you can.

Place the chickpeas, milk, soy cream, yeast flakes, stock powder, mustard, salt and pepper in a high-powered blender and whizz for 1 minute on high until silky smooth. Pour evenly over the potatoes. Sprinkle with the cheese and thyme leaves (if using).

Toss the breadcrumbs with a drizzle of extra virgin olive oil. Scatter over the top of everything. Finish with a sprinkle of salt and another crack of pepper.

Cover the dish with foil, poke 2 thin steam holes with a knife and bake for 1 hour. Poke in a fork to test whether the potato is cooked — if not, bake for another 10 minutes.

Remove the foil and grill for 5 minutes, or until the top is golden brown and bubbling.

Leave to sit for 5–10 minutes before serving — if you can!

### TIPS & SWAPS

- If you can't find soy cream, whizz ⅔ cup unsweetened plant-based milk and ⅓ cup neutral oil (such as grapeseed or sunflower) in a bullet or blender to combine — or use regular cream.
- You can omit the chickpeas if you like and it will still be delicious.

# SALADS

# ROASTED BEETROOT SALAD

**PREP** 20 minutes
**COOK** 1 hour 30 minutes
**SERVES** 4–5 as a side

- 6 beetroot (1.5kg / 3 lb 5 oz), trimmed
- ¼ cup extra virgin olive oil
- 8–10 fresh thyme sprigs
- 2 tsp liquid smoke (optional but delicious; see page 226)
- ½ cup crumbled feta (plant-based if preferred)
- chopped fresh mint or coriander
- pinch chilli flakes (optional)

**VINAIGRETTE**

- zest of 1 orange
- ¼ cup orange juice
- 3 tbsp extra virgin olive oil
- 2 tbsp lemon juice or red wine vinegar
- 1 tbsp maple syrup
- ½ tsp dijon mustard
- ½ tsp fresh thyme leaves, chopped
- ½ tsp salt
- cracked pepper

**NUTS**

- ¾ cup macadamia nuts
- 1 tbsp extra virgin olive oil
- 3 tbsp maple syrup

There's an air of sophistication to this salad. It celebrates the sweet, earthy beauty of the beetroot, which remains very much the star — but the lovely orangey vinaigrette enhances what's there and livens it all up with citrus tang. Don't even get me started on those candied macadamias, though. They're a wee bit scrumptious, so make sure you don't polish them off before the salad is served, okay?

To roast the beets, preheat the oven to 200°C (400°F) regular bake and line a casserole dish or deep roasting dish with baking paper.

Place the beets in the prepared dish, massage in the oil, then toss in the thyme. Season with salt and pepper all over. Drizzle with the liquid smoke (if using).

Lay a second sheet of baking paper over the dish (this helps stop steam escaping) and cover with the lid or a tight layer of foil. Bake for 1 hour 30 minutes, or until the beets are easily pierced with a sharp knife. Remove from the oven.

To make the orange vinaigrette, whisk the ingredients together in a small bowl and set aside.

When the beets are cool enough to handle, peel off and discard the skins (the flavour will have penetrated through to the beets). Cut the beets into thin round slices. Put them in a large bowl with half the vinaigrette. Toss gently to combine and set aside.

To make the candied nuts, put the macadamias in a small pan with the oil and fry over a medium-low heat, shaking the pan often, until golden all over. Add the maple syrup and cook for a couple of minutes until it's all sticky and caramelised and turning golden brown. Season with a little salt and pepper and transfer to a plate to cool down (the caramel will harden). Chop roughly before serving.

To assemble, arrange the beetroot slices slightly overlapping in a large shallow bowl or a platter. Drizzle with the remaining vinaigrette then scatter with the candied nuts, feta and herbs. Finish with a crack of black pepper, a small sprinkle of salt and a pinch of chilli flakes if you like.

# ZINGY POTATO SALAD

**PREP** 20 minutes
**COOK** 15 minutes
**SERVES** 4–5 as a side

- 1–1.25kg (2 lb 4 oz–2 lb 12 oz) baby new potatoes
- 4 gherkins, very finely sliced
- fresh dill sprigs, for garnish

**DRESSING**

- ½ cup extra virgin olive oil
- 3 shallots, finely chopped (about ½ cup)
- 2 cloves garlic, crushed
- 2 tbsp red wine vinegar
- 1 tbsp chopped capers (optional but yum)
- 1 tbsp wholegrain mustard
- 2 tsp dijon mustard
- 2 tsp maple syrup
- 1 tsp dried dill or 1 tbsp chopped fresh dill
- 2 tsp salt
- ½ tsp fine white pepper

This feels like a 'grown-up' potato salad — it may not be slathered in creamy mayo, but it's still satisfyingly luscious to eat. That mouthwatering, mustardy, garlicky vinaigrette is popping, and those are all the flavours that tasty little steamed potatoes just luuurve to wallow in. The fresh herbs add brightness and the gherkins and capers are punchy flavour heroes, too (you can easily omit them if they aren't your thing, though).

To make the dressing, combine the ingredients in a jug or shake in a glass jar. Leave to sit for at least half an hour to infuse.

To make the salad, boil or steam the potatoes in salted water until just tender, but not mushy. Keep checking the progress, and when they are done, drain well and return to the saucepan. While they're hot, add the dressing and toss to combine. Don't worry if a few potatoes break up a bit — that's nice.

Leave to cool to room temperature, then stir in the gherkins. Check the flavours and season to taste with salt and pepper if you think it needs it.

It's fine covered and left out for a few hours, and can be stored in a sealed container in the fridge for a couple of days. Serve at room temperature, topped with extra dill.

**TIPS & SWAPS**

- If you don't have baby new potatoes, you can use larger waxy potatoes and cut them in half.
- Use floury potatoes if you don't mind it all going a bit mushy.

# CREAMY MISO SLAW

**PREP** 30 minutes
**COOK** 5 minutes
**SERVES** 5–6 as a side

Here's a lovely new spin on a standard slaw — now you can turn up with something fresh and interesting next time you're asked to 'bring a salad'! It keeps well in the fridge so you can make it in advance, which is always a welcome perk. I've used tahini and miso here instead of mayo, which is a nice change-up.

6 cups finely shredded green and/or red cabbage
4 cups grated carrot
1 cup roasted salted peanuts, roughly chopped
½ cup chopped fresh coriander
¼ cup finely chopped fresh chives, plus extra for garnish
¼ cup toasted sesame seeds (optional)

**DRESSING**
5 tbsp hulled tahini
⅓ cup water
2 tbsp rice wine vinegar
2 tbsp toasted sesame oil
2 tbsp white (shiro) miso paste
1 tbsp maple syrup
2 tsp finely grated fresh ginger
1 clove garlic, crushed
¾ tsp salt
½ tsp fine black pepper

To make the dressing, place the ingredients in a bowl and whisk until creamy and smooth.

Place the cabbage, carrot, peanuts and herbs in a large mixing bowl. Pour in the dressing and toss to combine. Season with more salt and pepper if you think it needs it.

Refrigerate until ready to serve. You ideally want it sitting there for at least a few hours so the flavours have time to infuse.

Just before serving, transfer to a platter or bowl and scatter with extra chives and the sesame seeds (if using).

### TIPS & SWAPS

- You can use chopped roasted cashews or almonds or toasted sunflower seeds in place of the peanuts.

# MARINATED ZUCCHINI SALAD

**PREP** 20 minutes, plus 3+ hours marinating time

**COOK** 5 minutes

**SERVES** 4 as a side

700g (1 lb 9 oz) medium zucchini

½ cup pine nuts

250g (9 oz) cherry tomatoes, halved

¾ cup crumbled feta (plant-based if preferred)

¼ cup chopped fresh mint and/or dill

**MARINADE**

⅓ cup good-quality extra virgin olive oil

zest of 1 lemon

¼ cup lemon juice

2 tsp maple syrup

1 clove garlic, crushed

1 tbsp chopped fresh dill or ½ tsp dried dill

1 tsp finely chopped fresh oregano or ¼ tsp dried oregano

1¼ tsp salt

½ tsp fine black pepper

½ tsp dijon mustard

pinch chilli flakes

Summer 2024, my garden valiantly provided me with a constant supply of zucchini (courgettes), and I ended up pondering new ways to serve them that weren't fried, grilled, pickled, grated straight into a salad or made into zoodles (I love all those things, but still). Suddenly the idea of a simple yet elegant marinade seemed perfect — those lovely classic Greek flavours steep into the flesh, which *almost* pickles the strips a little bit so they're more tender when you eat them. Easy to prepare but oh so delectable and well balanced (salty feta, zingy zucchini and sweet tomatoes), this salad is perfection served alongside any summery meal, especially a barbecue.

Using a peeler, peel the zucchini into long strips. Use a bit of pressure so you get strips of a decent thickness. I prefer to discard the first-cut strips, which are mostly skin, and the soft, squishy seedy centre parts.

In a non-metallic bowl large enough to hold all the zucchini, whisk together the marinade ingredients. Add the zucchini and toss gently to combine. Cover and refrigerate for at least 3 hours, or up to 12 hours (give it a stir once while it's marinating).

When ready to serve, toast the pine nuts in a small, dry pan over a medium heat until just golden. Don't take your eyes off them — I mean it! Remove from the pan and chop roughly.

Toss the tomatoes through the zucchini then transfer everything to a shallow serving dish. Serve scattered with the feta, herbs and pine nuts, and seasoned with cracked pepper and a little salt if needed.

TIPS & SWAPS

- If you don't have cherry tomatoes, use chopped and deseeded regular tomatoes instead.

# CRUNCHY SALAD WITH CREAMY HERB DRESSING

**PREP** 30 minutes
**COOK** 8 minutes
**SERVES** 4–5 as a side

1 large or 2 small telegraph cucumbers
1 iceberg or cos lettuce or 2 baby cos lettuces, cut into wedges
1 large avocado, sliced or cubed

**CROUTONS**

3 slices artisan bread, such as sourdough or ciabatta
3 tbsp extra virgin olive oil

**CREAMY HERB DRESSING**

1 cup loosely packed chopped fresh soft herbs, such as chives, dill, mint, parsley, basil and/or coriander
½ cup hemp seeds or hearts
zest of 1 lemon
⅓ cup lemon juice
¼ cup water
¼ cup extra virgin olive oil
1 tbsp maple syrup
1 tsp dijon mustard
1 clove garlic, peeled
1¼ tsp salt
¼ tsp fine black pepper

**TO SERVE (OPTIONAL)**

fresh soft herbs
lemon juice
toasted hemp seeds

This is a delicious alternative to a traditional green salad. I love simple iceberg or cos lettuce done like this, with my take on a green-goddessy dressing (they were all the rage for years, and for good reason). I've used hemp seeds to make the dressing creamy, instead of cashews or mayo, because hemp seeds are LIFE (see page 226), but I've also added plenty of lemon and herbs so it's still zingy. Try to use as many of the stated soft herbs you can get your hands on, the more variety the better. If you'd rather thinly slice the cucumber crossways instead of lengthways, that's fine. You can skip the pickling step if you're in a rush but it adds a certain something for sure.

To make the croutons, preheat the oven to 180°C (350°F) fan bake. Tear or cut the bread into small bite-sized chunks (you should have about 2 cups of bread pieces) and place on a roasting tray. Drizzle with the oil and toss to coat. Season with salt and bake for about 8 minutes, or until golden brown and crunchy. Set aside.

To make the dressing, whizz the ingredients in a bullet or blender until smooth. Check the seasoning and adjust the salt, pepper and lemon to your liking if needed. Set aside in a jar in the fridge until needed.

Peel the cucumber into strips with a peeler or a mandolin if you have one, discarding the seedy bit in the middle. Place the strips in a bowl with a pinch of salt and a crack of pepper, and toss to combine. Set aside for 10 minutes, then squeeze the excess liquid out of the cucumber.

To assemble the salad, arrange the lettuce, cucumber and avocado on a serving dish. Scatter with the croutons and drizzle generously with the dressing. More fresh herbs, a squeeze of lemon and a sprinkle of toasted hemp seeds are nice touches, too.

**TIPS & SWAPS**

- Any leftover dressing will keep for a day or two in a jar in the fridge.

# ROASTED CAULIFLOWER & CHICKPEA SALAD

**PREP** 20 minutes
**COOK** 30 minutes
**SERVES** 5 as a side, 2–3 as a main

1 medium cauliflower

400g (14 oz) can chickpeas, drained (I prefer organic)

1 red onion, cut into eighths

½ cup Jungle Curry Paste (see page 212)

¼ cup extra virgin olive oil

3 cups baby spinach, washed

**DRESSING**

⅓ cup hulled tahini

¼ cup water

¼ cup finely chopped fresh coriander

zest of 1 lime or lemon

2 tbsp lime juice or 3 tbsp lemon juice, or to taste

1 clove garlic, crushed

¾ tsp salt

½ tsp fine black pepper

**TO SERVE (OPTIONAL)**

chopped fresh coriander

chilli flakes

lime or lemon zest and juice

Here's another way to use up that incredible Jungle Curry Paste you have left over — or a very good reason to make a fresh batch! And boy, does it take this cauliflower somewhere special. I mean, just roasting cauliflower by itself is transformative enough flavour-wise, so with this addition I'd go as far as to say it's all just a little bit magical — more so than it looks. This salad is quite robust so can be more of a meal than a side salad if you like, but it does go nicely alongside a protein when you've got hungry ones or you want something more filling.

Preheat the oven to 200°C (400°F) fan bake and line a large roasting tray with baking paper.

Cut the cauliflower into generous bite-sized florets (not too small or they'll go mushy) and transfer them to the prepared tray along with the chickpeas and onion. Add the Jungle Curry Paste and olive oil and use clean hands to toss it all around until evenly coated.

Bake for 30 minutes, or until everything is golden and the cauliflower is tender but not too soft. Remove from the oven.

While still hot, carefully transfer the contents of the roasting tray to a large mixing bowl and stir in the spinach — it will wilt a bit as it sits there.

To make the creamy dressing, whisk the ingredients together in a bowl or jug. Check the flavours and adjust the salt, pepper and lime or lemon juice until it tastes balanced to you.

To serve, arrange the cauliflower mixture on a platter and drizzle with the dressing. Finish with coriander, chilli flakes and lime or lemon zest if you like. An extra squeeze of lemon or lime can be good, too!

### TIPS & SWAPS

- If you like it milder, you could get away with only ⅓ cup Jungle Curry Paste.

# BIG ROASTY MEDITERRANEAN SALAD

**PREP** 20 minutes
**COOK** 35 minutes
**SERVES** 6

2 cups orzo (risoni) pasta (see tips for gluten-free)
2 tbsp vegetable stock powder
1 tsp salt
2 cups baby spinach, washed
2 tbsp finely chopped preserved lemon rind or 1 tbsp lemon zest
¾ cup chopped fresh soft herbs, such as coriander, dill, mint and/or parsley
½ cup sicilian or kalamata olives
¼ cup toasted pine nuts or flaked almonds
3–4 tbsp lemon juice, or to taste
¾ cup crumbled feta (plant-based if preferred)

**ROASTED STUFF**

300g (10½ oz) chorizo sausages (plant-based if preferred)
1 cup cherry tomatoes, halved
3 red capsicums, cut into 3–4cm (1¼–1½ in) chunks
2 red onions, cut into eighths
8 cloves garlic, peeled and sliced
1½ tbsp whole coriander seeds
1½ tbsp smoked paprika
1 tbsp coconut sugar
2 tsp salt
½ tsp fine black pepper
pinch chilli flakes
⅓ cup extra virgin olive oil

This is going to be a very popular dish, I just know it. There's something to be said for a salad where you can just shove a tray of stuff into the oven, waltz away, then later toss it (along with all its divinely roasted and intensified flavours) with a few other things and smugly serve! It's smart cooking to let the oven do the work. You're going to love the terrific variety of colours, flavours and textures — it all works together like a match made in culinary heaven. Good warm or cold, it's perfect for a potluck (brace yourself for compliments), as a light lunch by itself, or beside a protein for a family feast. You bet it'll be right at home on a barbecue table spread, too.

To prepare the roasted stuff, preheat the oven to 200°C (400°F) regular bake and line a baking tray with baking paper.

Place the whole sausages, tomatoes, capsicums, onions and garlic on the prepared tray. Sprinkle with the coriander seeds, smoked paprika, sugar, salt, pepper and chilli flakes. Add the olive oil and toss to combine evenly. Arrange in a single layer on the tray and roast for 35 minutes until tender but not too browned. Leave to cool a little.

While the sausages and veges are roasting, cook the pasta according to the packet directions, adding the stock powder and salt to the cooking water. Add the spinach at the very end to wilt. Drain well, then tip into a large serving bowl.

When the sausages are cool enough to handle, cut them into slices. Add them to the pasta, along with the whole tray of roasted stuff, including all the juices.

Add the preserved lemon or zest, herbs, olives, pine nuts or almonds and lemon juice and toss it all gently to combine. Season with more salt and lemon if you think it needs it.

Serve topped with feta and a crack of pepper.

### TIPS & SWAPS

- You can use 3 cups cooked brown or wild rice in place of the pasta for a gluten-free option.

# GRILLED SUMMERY SALAD

**PREP** 10 minutes
**COOK** 10 minutes
**SERVES** 4–6 as a side

- 2 red onions, quartered
- 3 zucchini, halved lengthways
- 2 red capsicums, cut in half and deseeded
- 2 corn cobs, husks and silks discarded
- extra virgin olive oil

**TO SERVE**

- ¼ cup chermoula (see page 218), or more to taste
- grilled halloumi or crumbled feta (optional)

If you haven't made my chermoula yet (see page 218), I'm here to tell you this is your sign! Truly, I just want everyone to experience the sheer magic of this wondrous condiment. It brings this simple summery salad to life and sets the ol' taste buds on fire with the incredible flavour it packs in! The salad itself couldn't be simpler to put together. If you have a barbecue on hand, by all means use this to grill the veges until they're tender and slightly charred. Otherwise, use the oven grill as specified below.

Preheat the oven grill or a barbecue grill to a high heat.

Arrange the onions, zucchini, capsicums and corn on a roasting tray and brush all over with olive oil. Season with salt and pepper.

Grill in the oven or on the barbecue for about 10 minutes until cooked but not too mushy (keep an eye on the zucchini, especially). It may not all turn golden and that's okay. You'll need to turn the corn a few times, but everything else just once.

To assemble the salad, separate the onions a little, roughly chop the zucchini and capsicums, and slice the corn kernels off the cobs. Place in a mixing bowl.

While still fairly hot, add the chermoula, then toss to combine. Check the flavours, and if you feel like it could do with a little more chermoula, stir a bit more through.

Either serve as it is, or jazz it up with the halloumi or feta for a more robust salad.

### TIPS & SWAPS

- If you have a gas hob, you can run the oven-grilled corn quickly through the flame to blacken it slightly and add a barbecue flavour.

# TABBOULEH

**PREP** 40 minutes
**COOK** 15 minutes
**SERVES** 6 as a side

400g (14 oz) pearl couscous
1 tbsp vegetable stock powder
½ cup roughly chopped pistachios or pumpkin or sunflower seeds
3 tomatoes, cut into 1cm (½ in) dice
1 small cucumber (170g / 5¾ oz), cut into 1cm (½ in) dice
1 bunch spring onions, finely sliced on an angle
2 cups loosely packed finely chopped fresh parsley
1 cup loosely packed finely chopped fresh mint
2 tsp sumac (optional)
zest of 1 lemon
1 tsp salt
1 tsp fine black pepper

**VINAIGRETTE**

½ cup extra virgin olive oil
¼ cup lemon juice
1 tbsp maple syrup
1½ tsp ground cumin
1 tsp salt
1 clove garlic, crushed

**TO SERVE (OPTIONAL)**

½ cup pomegranate seeds (arils)
1 preserved lemon, flesh discarded, rind finely diced
extra sumac

This classic, stunningly fresh and flavoursome salad is hugely popular for good reason. It's stunning served next to a protein as a simple meal, or proudly proffered as a bring-along for a potluck dinner or part of a summery barbecue spread. Or you can make it as part of a more opulent Middle Eastern feast (alongside crispy falafel, chermoula and fresh pita, which are all recipes in this book). I've used pearl (Israeli) couscous as the base here because I love the texture, but regular couscous works, as does cooked quinoa for gluten-free. Or you can use cooked or soaked bulgur wheat (which is the most traditional grain to use).

Cook the couscous according to the packet directions, adding the stock powder to the water. Drain, toss with a little olive oil and set aside. Allow to cool fully before making the salad.

Preheat the oven to 180°C (350°F) regular bake. Place the nuts or seeds on a small tray and roast for about 6 minutes, until slightly golden and fragrant. Give them a stir partway through if you like.

Toss the tomatoes and cucumber in a bowl with 1 tsp salt and leave to sit for at least 10 minutes. Drain off and discard the liquid.

To make the vinaigrette, place the ingredients in a bowl or jug and whisk to combine.

To assemble the salad, place the cooled couscous in a large serving bowl. Add the drained tomato and cucumber, spring onions, herbs, sumac (if using), lemon zest, salt and pepper. Add the vinaigrette and toss to combine.

If you like, the tabbouleh can be served immediately — but it gets tastier if you let it rest for at least 30 minutes to allow the flavours to come together.

Serve sprinkled with the chopped nuts or seeds and topped with your choice of the pomegranate seeds, preserved lemon and/or extra sumac.

**TIPS & SWAPS**

- For another gluten-free option in place of the couscous, you could pulse half a medium cauliflower in a food processor to make 'rice'. No need to cook it.
- You can use halved cherry tomatoes instead of the regular tomatoes if you have them.

# SWEETS

# BIGBOG BROWNIES

**PREP** 10 minutes
**COOK** 20–25 minutes
**SERVES** 25 pieces

- 2 tbsp ground flaxseed
- 5 tbsp cold water
- ¾ cup chickpea flour
- ½ cup flour or gluten-free flour blend (see page 222)
- 1 cup coconut sugar
- ½ cup dark cocoa powder
- ½ tsp baking powder
- ½ tsp salt
- ¼ tsp baking soda
- ½ cup almond butter or hulled tahini
- ½ cup rice syrup
- ½ cup plant-based milk
- ⅓ cup coconut oil
- 1 tbsp pure vanilla extract
- ¼ cup sugar-free, plant-based dark chocolate chips or chopped chocolate (optional)

This is the ultimate fridge brownie — gooey, fudgy, rich and sweet, but not sickening, and definitely best served chilled. I had my work cut out for me because what gives a traditional brownie that decadent fudge texture is a bucket of white sugar. And that's all very well when you're young and carefree, but not ideal when you have kids who rain terror upon the household as a result of ingesting said sugar. Turns out, I nailed it with a miraculous combination of wondrous ingredients (including chickpea flour, which I adore). It took me ages. But here it is, dedicated to my friends Andrea and Dave, who instructed me to create this one back when all I had was a mess of half-finished recipes and a dream. Don't even ask what 'bigbog' means — it's a long story involving autocorrect (a story that's actually not that funny unless you're kind of immature, like me).

Preheat the oven to 190°C (375°F) regular bake and line the base and sides of a 20cm (8 in) square slice tin with baking paper.

Stir the flaxseed and water together in a mug or small bowl and set aside for 5–10 minutes to thicken. Stir again before use.

Sift the flours, sugar, cocoa, baking powder, salt and baking soda into a medium mixing bowl and stir to combine.

Place the almond butter or tahini, rice syrup, milk, coconut oil and vanilla in a small saucepan. Warm over a low heat, stirring constantly, until just melted (don't let it simmer or boil).

Add the milk mixture and the flaxseed mixture to the dry ingredients and stir to combine. It will go quite thick — this is okay.

Transfer to the prepared tin and flatten it out with a damp spatula or clean, damp fingers. Sprinkle with the chocolate (if using).

Bake for 20–25 minutes. You want it just undercooked — if it's overcooked, it will be dry. A toothpick or skewer poked in shouldn't come out too clean. Every oven is different so it's hard to say exactly how long it needs, but you'll figure out the sweet spot after you've made it a few times.

Allow to cool completely in the tin, then refrigerate for an hour or two before slicing. Extra delicious with a dollop of whipped plant-based cream.

Store in an airtight container in the fridge so it stays chewy and gooey.

# OATY PEANUT BUTTER CHOCOLATE CHIP COOKIES

**PREP** 30 minutes
**COOK** 12–14 minutes
**MAKES** about 12

½ cup crunchy peanut butter
½ cup coconut sugar
¼ cup maple syrup
1 ripe banana, mashed
1 tsp pure vanilla extract
¼ tsp salt
2 cups rolled oats (see tip)
1 cup ground almonds
½ tsp baking soda, sifted
¼ tsp ground cinnamon
½ cup sugar-free, plant-based chocolate chips or chopped chocolate

I feel compelled to warn you that these cookies are as addictive as they are simple to make. A dangerous combo! There are always one or two recipes from a book that get me like that and this is one of them; it's difficult to eat them in singles. And with that flavour combo, who'd be surprised? It's basically a no-fail, one-bowl wonder and will probably become a regular in your kitchen if you're baking for lunchboxes. I use sugar-free chocolate drops from the supermarket so the boys don't ping off the walls, or even raisins or chopped dried apricots for a toned-down, more healthful (but still scrumptious) rendition.

Preheat the oven to 180°C (350°F) regular bake and line two baking trays with baking paper.

Place the peanut butter, coconut sugar, maple syrup, banana, vanilla and salt in a medium mixing bowl and stir to combine.

Whizz the rolled oats in a food processor until they're semi-blended; you want a variety of larger chunks and finer flour. Transfer to a large mixing bowl and add the ground almonds, baking soda, cinnamon and chocolate. Mix well.

Add the peanut butter mixture to the dry ingredients and stir with a wooden spoon or a fork to combine into an even doughy batter. If it gets too hard to mix, you can always use your clean hands.

Roll into about 12 golf-ball-sized balls. Place on the prepared trays and squash flat with a fork or the palm of your hand, so they're 1–2cm (½–¾ in) high.

Bake for 12–14 minutes, or until golden brown all over. If they're not quite there, put them back in for 2 minutes but keep an eye on them.

Allow to stand on the tray for 5–10 minutes before transferring to a wire rack to cool. When completely cool, store in an airtight container in the pantry (or tightly sealed in the freezer for a couple of months).

### TIPS & SWAPS

- If you can't eat peanuts, use almond butter instead. You could add a few finely chopped almonds for texture.
- You can use whizzed-up sunflower seeds instead of the ground almonds if you prefer.
- If you can't eat oats, use quinoa flakes instead.

# AFGHANS

**PREP** 20 minutes, plus 1 hour setting time

**COOK** 11 minutes

**MAKES** 18

1 cup flour or gluten-free flour blend (see page 222)
½ cup buckwheat flour
1 cup coconut sugar
½ cup cocoa powder
½ cup ground almonds
⅓ cup desiccated coconut
½ tsp salt
¾ cup coconut oil, melted but not hot
¼ cup plant-based milk
¼ cup maple syrup
2 tsp pure vanilla extract
3 cups cornflakes

**ICING**

¾ cup cashew, almond or sunflower butter
⅔ cup maple syrup or agave syrup
½ cup cocoa powder
2 tsp pure vanilla extract
½ tsp salt
3 tbsp coconut milk

**TO DECORATE**

whole or half walnuts

It's hard to believe that it's been five cookbooks since I've featured an afghan recipe; it was high time I revisited this essential Kiwi classic. As I've always said, they were my preferred tuck-shop treat back in the day. I liked them more than cream doughnuts, and I'd still find it hard to choose, if I'm honest (maybe it's those cornflakes). These are very decadent and chocolatey to eat (as if you couldn't tell by looking at the photo) but a whole lot better for you than most – meaning you can eat more of them! Makes sense, right? It does in my head.

Preheat the oven to 170°C (325°F) regular bake and line a baking tray with baking paper (you may need two trays).

Place the flours, coconut sugar, cocoa, ground almonds, coconut and salt in a large mixing bowl and stir to combine.

Add the coconut oil, milk, maple or agave syrup and vanilla, then stir with a wooden spoon or spatula to bring it all together.

Lastly mix through the cornflakes – I just use my clean hands to do this and give it a good hard scrunch. (If you're using organic cornflakes, you'll need to pre-scrunch them as they don't break as easily.)

With damp hands, tightly squish the dough into golf-ball-sized balls or discs. Arrange on the baking tray/s and use a fork to gently press them down halfway, as they won't rise or spread in the oven.

Bake for 15 minutes, then leave to cool completely before icing – they will be fragile when warm.

To make the icing, place the nut butter, syrup, cocoa, vanilla and salt in a small bowl and stir with a whisk or fork to combine. If you think it needs thinning, add 1 tbsp coconut cream at a time until it's the desired consistency.

Ice the cooled cookies by blobbing icing on with a teaspoon and smearing it out a bit. Top each with a walnut.

Store in an airtight container – you can also refrigerate them if you like them super firm.

## TIPS & SWAPS

- You can use all plain flour if you like, just add an extra 1 tbsp each of coconut oil and maple syrup.
- For a nut-free version, use finely whizzed up sunflower seeds in place of the ground almonds and sunflower butter in the icing. Omit the walnut, too.

# BREAKFAST COOKIES

**PREP** 15 minutes
**COOK** 13–15 minutes
**MAKES** about 15

I love these cookies so much. As well as being perfect for a cheeky morning bite on the go, they seem to make excellent fodder for new mums. A friend made them for me for Sage's birth, and they were one of the first things I ate (along with some fruit) after he was born. I've since made them for my friends to celebrate their own special moment. That being said, they'll suit anyone at any time and are worth the prep that goes into them. Best of all, the recipe is fairly flexible in terms of what nuts, seeds and dried fruit you put in — choose what you like and have a play with the ratios. Bake them in batches so you can figure out the right cooking time for your oven, depending on what texture you like.

- 2 tbsp ground flaxseed
- 5 tbsp cold water
- 1 cup flour or gluten-free flour blend (see page 222)
- ¾ cup shredded coconut
- ½ heaped cup quinoa flakes or fine rolled oats
- ½ cup ground almonds
- ¼ cup coconut sugar
- ¼ cup hemp seeds
- 2 tsp ground cinnamon
- 1 tsp ground ginger
- 1 tsp baking powder
- 1 tsp baking soda
- ½ tsp salt
- ½ cup nut butter, such as peanut, almond and/or cashew butter
- ½ cup maple syrup and/or rice malt syrup
- ¼ cup hulled tahini
- ¼ cup melted coconut oil
- 2 tsp pure vanilla extract
- 1 heaped cup mixed seeds and nuts, such as pumpkin or sunflower seeds, chopped almonds and/or walnuts
- ¾ cup dried fruit, such as raisins, apricots, currants

Preheat the oven to 190°C (375°F) regular bake and line one or two baking trays with baking paper.

Stir the flaxseed and water together in a mug or small bowl and set aside for 5–10 minutes to thicken. Stir again before use.

Place the flour, coconut, quinoa or oats, ground almonds, sugar, hemp, cinnamon, ginger, baking powder, baking soda and salt in a large mixing bowl and stir to combine.

Place the nut butter, maple or rice syrup, tahini, coconut oil and vanilla in a smaller mixing bowl. Add the flaxseed mixture and stir with a whisk to combine evenly.

Scrape the wet mixture into the dry ingredients and stir with a spatula or wooden spoon. Just before the dough is combined, stir in the nuts, seeds and dried fruit.

Roll the dough into golf-ball-sized balls and flatten each into a cookie shape on the prepared tray using a fork or moistened fingers. They will puff up slightly in the oven.

Bake for about 13 minutes, or until golden all over. Cool completely before storing in an airtight container.

These cookies keep in the freezer, well-sealed, for up to a month. And they go nice and chewy!

# MINT-AS SLICE

**PREP** 1 hour, plus 7+ hours setting time

**COOK** 18 minutes

**MAKES** about 20 pieces

### BASE

- 1 cup flour or gluten-free flour blend (see page 222 or use store-bought)
- ¾ cup coconut sugar
- ½ cup desiccated coconut
- ⅓ cup dark cocoa powder
- ½ tsp baking powder
- ¼ tsp salt
- ½ cup melted coconut oil
- ¼ cup plant-based milk
- 2 tbsp rice syrup

### FILLING

- 250g (9 oz) cacao butter or cocoa butter, finely chopped
- ¾ cup UHT coconut cream (I use the Kara brand)
- ½ cup agave syrup or maple syrup
- 1 tbsp peppermint essence
- ½ tsp salt
- ⅓ cup fresh mint leaves (optional but amazing)

### TOPPING

- ⅓ cup coconut oil
- ⅓ cup pure maple syrup
- 2 tbsp rice syrup
- ½ tsp peppermint essence
- ⅓ cup dark cocoa powder

### TIPS & SWAPS

- The filling sets to a much better consistency using UHT coconut cream from a carton (I use the Kara brand). You can use Kara *canned* coconut cream, but only if using a blender – or it won't set. You can use a food processor on high for the filling as long as you use UHT coconut cream.
- If you're using my gluten-free flour mix you will only need ¾ cup.

If only you knew how much time and energy has gone into making this seemingly innocent confection. Leaving out the icing sugar turned out to be a lot more difficult than expected (long and frustrating story featuring many a grainy filling), so when I finally figured out the trick, it was a legitimate eureka moment and now I know how Einstein must have felt. I was determined not to use cashews either, so it was cacao butter that turned out to be the absolute star of this show – and boy, it makes it super special. You probably won't find it at the supermarket but grab some from your local specialty food store, bulk food store or refillery (or order it online), because this slice is utterly divine and tastes just like a Mint Treat – but better, obvs. See page 227 for the down-low on cacao butter.

Preheat the oven to 180°C (350°F) regular bake and line the base and sides of a 20cm (8 in) square slice tin with baking paper.

To make the base, place the flour, sugar, coconut, cocoa, baking powder and salt in a bowl and stir gently with a whisk to combine. Mix the coconut oil, milk and rice syrup in another bowl. Add to the dry ingredients and stir to combine into a firm batter. Use a spatula to smush it into the prepared tin in an even layer.

Bake for 18 minutes, then allow to cool completely.

To make the filling, place the cacao or cocoa butter in a heatproof bowl sitting over a saucepan of simmering water and stir until melted. Transfer to a pouring jug and allow to cool to room temperature, or lukewarm. If it cools too much it will start to harden again, but you can always re-melt it. It needs to be clear, not cloudy.

If you have a blender that can run on a medium-low speed, you can use this to mix it all up – otherwise use a food processor on its highest speed.

Place the coconut cream, agave or maple syrup, peppermint essence and salt in the blender or food processor. Start the motor and, while it's running, very slowly pour in the melted cacao or cocoa butter in the thinnest stream you can. It will require patience on your part! Continue to pour slowly until it's two-thirds gone, then you can pour faster as it will start to thicken up. Stop the motor once it's used up.

Lastly, add the mint leaves (if using) and whizz for a few seconds on high until finely chopped. Pour the mixture over the cooled biscuit base, shimmy it out evenly, then cover and refrigerate for about 6 hours or overnight until set. It will take much longer to set if you've used canned coconut cream.

To make the topping, place all the ingredients except the cocoa in a heatproof bowl sitting over a saucepan of gently simmering water (but not touching the water). Add a pinch of salt and stir until melted, then remove the bowl from the heat and whisk until everything is evenly combined.

Add the cocoa and stir briskly with the whisk until smooth. Pour over the top of the mint layer and swirl it out to coat the whole thing. Refrigerate for about an hour until set.

Slice into squares and store in an airtight container in the fridge (they will last for a week or so), or keep them in the freezer and take one out when you feel like it. They remind me of little ice cream bites this way!

# HELIENA'S CARAMEL SLICE

**PREP** 1 hour, plus 7+ hours setting time

**COOK** 15 minutes

**MAKES** about 20 pieces

**BASE**

- 1¼ cups flour or gluten-free flour blend (see page 222)
- 1 cup ground almonds
- ½ cup shredded coconut
- ¼ cup coconut sugar
- ½ tsp salt
- ¼ tsp baking powder
- ½ cup coconut oil
- ½ cup brown rice syrup
- 1 tsp pure vanilla extract or paste

**CARAMEL**

- 2 x 400ml (14 fl oz) cans full-fat coconut cream
- 1 cup coconut sugar
- ⅓ cup store-bought date paste
- ½ cup cashew butter
- ⅓ cup brown rice syrup or coconut nectar
- 1 tbsp pure vanilla extract or paste
- ¾ tsp salt
- 6 tbsp cornflour mixed with 4 tbsp water to make a slurry

**TOPPING**

- ⅔ cup coconut oil
- ⅔ cup agave syrup or maple syrup
- 1 tbsp brown rice syrup
- 1 tsp pure vanilla extract
- ⅔ cup cocoa or cacao powder

This slice has literally been years in the making. My cherished (and very clever) friend Heliena and I have been chipping away diligently on various versions of it, both with the same dream in mind — sweet, nostalgic, fully fledged decadence without compromise, but free of refined sugar and gluten. Oh, and plant-based. Seems impossible, I know. Sharing notes, discussing how certain ingredients behaved with different methods ... it's been a labour of love, I can tell you. Ultimately it was she who mastered it in the end; I merely swooped in and tweaked it for this book. The result? Jubilation for the soul. Rapturous delight in every mouthful. A perfect balance of firm, cakey chew, luxurious caramel and rich chocolate. I'm afraid I can't emphasise just how good it is using the feeble written word — you simply must try it for yourself.

**BASE**

Preheat the oven to 180°C (350°F) regular bake and line the base and sides of a 20cm (8 in) square slice tin with baking paper.

Combine the flour, ground almonds, coconut, coconut sugar, salt and baking powder in a mixing bowl. Melt the coconut oil in a small saucepan. Remove from the heat, add the rice syrup and vanilla, stir, then add to the dry ingredients. Use a wooden spoon or clean wet hands to combine everything into a dough. Press evenly into the prepared tin (the back of a dessertspoon helps to get it smooth and even).

Bake for 15 minutes, until only a very pale golden all over. Allow to cool.

**CARAMEL**

While the base is cooking, start the caramel. Place the coconut cream and coconut sugar in a large saucepan, set over a medium heat and wait for it to melt and begin to simmer gently. Turn the heat down and leave it on a gentle rolling simmer for 20 minutes (set a timer), stirring occasionally. Using my gas hob, I start on medium but once it starts simmering I reduce it to the lowest heat setting. For induction, the lowest setting will probably be too low, so just look for the rolling simmer — not boiling its head off.

After 20 minutes, stir in the date paste and simmer for another 7 minutes. Add the cashew butter, rice syrup or coconut nectar, vanilla and salt, and stir gently with a whisk until the cashew butter is all incorporated (it might take a few minutes). Remove from the heat.

Stir the slurry together, then drizzle into the caramel while stirring all the time. Return to a low heat for gas (or medium-low for induction) and stir very gently until all of a sudden the mixture thickens — going from a thin sauce consistency to that of a thick custard or pudding. It will take 1–5 minutes. As soon as it's thick and ribbons of caramel form when they fall from the spoon, remove it from the heat immediately. You don't want to let it get too hot or boil, or it will split.

Pour the caramel onto the cooled base and jiggle the tin to smooth it out. Allow to cool for 30 minutes, then cover and refrigerate for 6 hours or overnight to set (overnight is better for slicing).

Recipe continued on next page

#### TOPPING

Place the coconut oil, agave or maple syrup, rice syrup and vanilla in a heatproof bowl sitting over a saucepan of simmering water. When melted, remove from the heat and whisk to combine evenly. Add the cocoa and a pinch of salt and stir briskly with the whisk until smooth.

#### TO ASSEMBLE

Pour the topping over the set caramel and refrigerate for at least an hour to set. When set, slice with a sharp knife.

Store in an airtight container in the fridge for up to 10 days. It gets better with time – although I'll eat my hat if it lasts that long.

You can also cut the slice into small pieces and freeze them (well-sealed) for up to a month. They're sublime eaten straight from the freezer.

#### TIPS & SWAPS

- If you can't find premade date paste, make your own by soaking 300g (10½ oz) pitted regular dates in just-boiled water for 10 minutes. Drain, then whizz in a food processor, scraping down the sides often, until it finally catches. Whizz until smooth. Use ½ cup of this paste in the caramel (it's a lot softer than the store-bought stuff).
- For a nut-free version, use ¾ cup finely whizzed sunflower seeds instead of the ground almonds in the base, and hulled tahini instead of the cashew butter in the caramel.

# CUSTARD SQUARES

**PREP** 1 hour, plus 6+ hours setting time

**COOK** 20 minutes

**MAKES** about 10 pieces

### PASTRY

- 2 sheets flaky puff pastry (plant-based if preferred)
- ¼ cup aquafaba (the liquid from canned chickpeas) or a beaten free-range egg

### CUSTARD

- ½ cup + 1 tbsp custard powder
- 2½ cups creamy plant-based milk (I use soy milk)
- 500ml (17 fl oz) coconut cream
- ½ cup + 2 tbsp agave syrup (for less sweet) or maple syrup
- ¾ tsp salt
- ¼ tsp ground turmeric (optional, for colour)
- 1½ tbsp vanilla paste

### ICING

- ⅓ cup coconut oil
- ⅓ cup maple syrup
- ⅓ cup cocoa powder

Remember the now-famous custard square from *Homemade Happiness*? It kinda took the country by storm, without any exaggeration. Since then I've always wanted to create a plant-based version, and now you've got the added bonus of it being free of refined sugar, which is the cherry on top! I can guarantee you it's still sweet, rich and gratifyingly creamy (you know I wouldn't lead you astray). The pre-baked pastry creates a flutter of crispy layers in contrast to that luscious custard, so while they're fresh, every mouthful feels like an exquisite celebration of texture. (I still love them once they've gone a lil' soggy, though, which they will.) It's worth the little extra expense of using vanilla paste rather than extract, as it does make a difference to the overall flavour. See the tips for a gluten-free option.

### PASTRY

Preheat the oven to 190°C (375°F) fan bake and line a 21cm (8¼ in) square slice tin with a couple of pieces of clingfilm so it goes all the way up the sides. Have two baking trays ready — one for the pastry to sit on and one to sit on top to stop it puffing up. Tear two pieces of baking paper just larger than the pastry.

Place one sheet of paper on a baking tray, place a sheet of pastry on top and prick it a few times with a fork. Top with the other sheet of paper then the other baking tray. Bake for 17 minutes if using plant-based pastry, or 14 minutes if using butter pastry.

Remove the top tray, brush the top of the pastry with the aquafaba or beaten egg (this helps seal it) and cook uncovered for another few minutes. Check it. Is it a deep golden brown all over? Put it back in if it's not.

Set the cooked pastry sheet carefully aside to cool while you repeat the process with the other pastry sheet.

If your pastry sheets are bigger than your tin, lay one sheet on a board and sit the tin on top. Cut around the base of the tin with a sharp knife so the pastry will fit nicely inside the tin. Place the pastry in the base of the prepared tin with the sealed side up. Repeat with the other pastry sheet and set that one aside.

### CUSTARD

Place the custard powder in a jug, add ½ cup of the milk and stir with a fork or small whisk to make a smooth slurry.

Transfer to a medium saucepan and add the remaining milk, coconut cream and the agave or maple syrup, salt and turmeric (if using). Cook over a medium heat, stirring gently with a whisk, until it's a very thick pudding consistency (5–10 minutes). Don't leave it unattended because it can thicken quite suddenly.

Stir the vanilla paste through the custard. Transfer it to a mixing bowl and allow to cool at room temperature for about 15 minutes, whisking every few minutes to stop a skin forming (don't let it cool right down or it will start setting). Then give it another good whisk to smooth out any lumps.

Spread the custard onto the bottom layer of pastry in the tin. Press the other piece of pastry on top (sealed-side down), and refrigerate for at least 6 hours or overnight. You can ice it after it's been in the fridge for an hour or two.

Recipe continued on next page

## ICING

Gently melt the coconut oil in a bowl sitting over a small saucepan of simmering water. Add the maple syrup and whisk to combine evenly. Remove from the heat, add the cocoa and a pinch of salt and whisk until just combined.

Pour the icing on top of the pastry in the tin, spread out with the back of a spoon and return to the fridge for at least another 20 minutes to set.

When set, place the slice on a clean board and, using a sharp serrated knife, slice it into long sections lengthways. Turn each section onto its side and cut it into pieces from the side so you don't squash it. Cover and keep refrigerated until serving. It will keep for a couple of days in a sealed container in the fridge.

### TIPS & SWAPS

- Many brands of store-bought puff pastry sheets are 'accidentally' dairy-free as they contain vegetable oils rather than butter – check the ingredients.
- For a gluten-free version, use store-bought pre-rolled gluten-free puff pastry. Bake uncovered at 200°C (400°F) fan bake for 10 minutes, press down with a tray to get all the air out, then bake for 2 minutes until golden all over. There's no need to brush with aquafaba or a beaten egg – it's important you cut the gluten-free pastry to shape while it's still warm.
- If you like your custard a little more gooey, try using 1 tbsp less custard powder.

# CUSTARD CREAM DOUGHNUTS

**PREP** 1 hour, plus 2–3 hours rising time

**COOK** 20 minutes

**MAKES** 12

### DOUGHNUTS

- ½ cup water
- 1½ tsp active yeast granules
- ¼ cup + 1 tsp coconut sugar or muscovado sugar
- 2 cups high-grade or baker's flour
- 1 cup flour (I use organic unbleached)
- 1 tsp salt
- 3 tbsp coconut oil, melted but not hot
- ¼ cup pumpkin purée (see tip)
- ½ cup plant-based milk (or regular milk)

### CUSTARD CREAM

- ⅓ cup custard powder
- 1¼ cups milk or plant-based milk (I use creamy soy milk)
- 250ml (9 fl oz) coconut cream (I use the Kara brand in a carton)
- ¼ cup + 3 tbsp agave syrup or ½ cup maple syrup
- 2 tsp vanilla paste (or extract)
- ½ tsp salt
- ⅛ tsp ground turmeric (optional, for colour)
- ½ cup plant-based whipping cream (or regular cream)

### TO COOK & ASSEMBLE

- ½ cup coconut sugar (or icing sugar)
- neutral oil, such as grapeseed, sunflower or rice bran oil, for frying
- dark berry jam (sugar-free if preferred)

Get a load of these, will ya! My mouth waters gazing at this image. All the cream doughnut goodness without the dairy or eggs! It was a little work on my part to get them here but lo, raise your arms to the heavens, they're a triumph! The little bit of pumpkin in the dough makes for a lovely, soft cakey texture and the high-grade flour will ensure a nice bit of chew on the fried outside, a little bit of crispy, too! The custard cream is next-level decadence and that splodge of gooey jam adds the tang it needs to finish. Yup, making doughnuts is always a process, but a very satisfying one that's well worth the effort.

### CUSTARD CREAM

Prep the custard in advance, or while the dough is rising, and keep it in the fridge until needed. Place the custard powder in a mug with ¼ cup of the milk. Stir with a fork or small whisk to make a smooth slurry.

Place the remaining milk in a saucepan with the coconut cream, agave syrup, custard powder slurry, vanilla, salt and turmeric (if using). Cook over a medium heat, stirring with a whisk, for 5–8 minutes until it thickens to a very thick pudding consistency. Best not to leave it unattended because it can thicken quite suddenly. Transfer to a bowl, cover and refrigerate for an hour or two until firm.

When ready to serve, whip the whipping cream until thick (using an electric beater is easiest). Remove the custard from the fridge and use an electric beater to beat it on high until mostly smooth. Add the whipped cream to the custard and fold to combine. Transfer to a piping bag or a zip-lock bag with the corner snipped off. Pop the bag in the fridge until you're ready to assemble the doughnuts.

### TO MAKE THE DOUGHNUTS

Whisk together the water, yeast and 1 tsp of the coconut sugar or muscovado sugar in a small bowl or jug. Set aside for 5–10 minutes until it 'blooms' (goes frothy).

Place the remaining ¼ cup coconut sugar or muscovado sugar in a large mixing bowl with the flours and salt. Make a well in the centre and pour in the coconut oil, pumpkin purée, milk and frothy yeast mixture. Stir with a wooden spoon until it comes together into a craggy dough.

Tip the craggy mass onto a clean, lightly floured benchtop and start to knead. It may start off sticky but eventually firm up, so just keep going, folding the dough over and pressing it out hard away from you with the palm of one hand, bringing it around a quarter-turn, then folding it over and pressing it out again. (Google how to knead properly if you're unsure.) Knead for about 15 minutes. By the end the dough should be smooth, and stretchy enough that when you pull a piece off, you can stretch it out with your fingertips into a thin square or 'screen' that you can see light through — and you should be a bit puffed! You can also use the dough hook of a stand mixer on a low speed for 5 minutes, but usually I end up finishing it off by hand.

Wash and lightly oil the mixing bowl. Place the dough ball back in the bowl, cover with a clean, damp tea towel and put it in a warmish, draught-free place, such as a hot water cupboard or a warm room. I put mine, uncovered, in the turned-off oven with a bowl of just-boiled water.

Recipe continued on next page

Allow to rise until it doubles in size. This will take anywhere from 1 to 3 hours.

At this point, you can knock the dough right back down again with your fist, cover with clingfilm and leave in the fridge overnight if you want to (I love this method).

Gently knead the dough again for about 30 seconds (let it come to room temperature first if it's been in the fridge). Divide the dough into two pieces (if you have electronic scales, it helps to use them to divide the portions equally, but it's not essential). Place one half back in the bowl and cover it.

Roll the other half into a sausage and cut into 6 even pieces. Firmly roll each piece on the bench until it forms a smooth ball shape. It may take some time. Having very lightly greased hands helps. Repeat with the remaining dough so you have 12 balls.

Line two baking trays with lightly greased baking paper and arrange the dough balls on top with room in between for them to double in size. Cut the baking paper so each ball is sitting on its own piece, with lots of room to expand.

Place the trays in the turned-off oven with a bowl of just-boiled water. Leave for about 30 minutes — they won't quite double in size now, but they'll finish puffing up when fried. If they overproof now, they'll collapse at that point. Be VERY gentle with them now. Don't touch them.

#### TO COOK THE DOUGHNUTS

Gently remove the trays from the oven. Set a wire rack over paper towels.

Place the coconut sugar in a bullet or food processor and whizz to a finer grain. Place in a wide bowl ready for coating the doughnuts.

Heat about 7cm (2¾ in) oil in a medium saucepan over a medium heat. The oil needs to reach 180°C (350°F). (If you don't have a thermometer, wait until handle of a wooden spoon bubbles rapidly when dipped in the oil.) Carefully lower a doughnut into the oil and cook until deep golden brown before turning and cooking the other side. If your oil is at the right temperature this should take about 90 seconds each side — if they brown too quickly turn the heat down, or off then on again.

#### TO ASSEMBLE THE DOUGHNUTS

Remove from the oil using a slotted spoon and place on the wire rack to drain. Dredge in the sugar while still warm. You can keep the unfilled doughnuts in an airtight container at room temperature for a day.

When completely cold, slice the top of each doughnut open with a serrated knife to make a pocket for the custard cream. Pipe in the custard cream and dollop generously with jam. Dust with more sugar to serve.

#### TIPS & SWAPS

- To make the pumpkin purée, steam about 250g (9 oz) pumpkin pieces until tender, then remove the skin and mash or purée. If you don't eat pumpkin, use the same amount of apple sauce / apple purée. Allow to cool completely before using.
- Always check the expiry date on yeast before use — it won't work if it is old.
- You can use regular or golden icing sugar instead of the coconut sugar for the coating if preferred.

# DREAMY APRICOT SHORTCAKE

**PREP** 20 minutes, plus 40 minutes soaking time

**COOK** 35–40 minutes

**MAKES** 16–20 pieces

**BASE**

- 1 tbsp ground flaxseed
- 3 tbsp water
- 2 cups flour or gluten-free flour blend (see page 222)
- 1 cup ground almonds
- 1 cup coconut sugar
- ¾ cup shredded coconut
- 1 tsp baking powder
- ½ tsp salt
- ⅔ cup coconut oil
- ⅓ cup maple syrup
- ¼ cup plant-based milk
- 2 tsp pure vanilla extract

**TOPPING**

- ⅓ cup chopped walnuts or flaked almonds

**FILLING**

- 3 cups (500g / 1 lb 2 oz) whole dried apricots
- 1 cup apricot jam (sugar-free if preferred)
- ⅓ cup brown rice syrup
- 5 tbsp cornflour mixed with 3 tbsp water to make a slurry
- 1 tbsp pure vanilla extract
- 1 tbsp lemon juice

Favourite recipe in this book? At the time of writing, yes. Words cannot express how enamoured I am. Everything about it makes me feel elated and rosy with appreciation – the sweet, slightly tart, unctuous gooeyness of the apricot layer, the wholesome, almost cake-like texture of the base, the creamy earthiness of walnuts, and the toasted coconut flavour nudging in pleasantly. I keep it in a container in my fridge. I sensibly take a single piece to enjoy with my cup of tea in the evenings (while I catch an episode of whatever series I'm currently hooked on), and invariably end up making about three separate – mildly shameful – trips back to the kitchen for more. You have been warned.

Preheat the oven to 180°C (350°F) regular bake and line the base and sides of a 21cm (8¼ in) square slice tin with baking paper.

To presoak the apricots, place them in a heatproof bowl and cover with just-boiled water. Soak for 40 minutes (time this), then drain.

To make the base, stir the flaxseed and water together in a mug or small bowl and set aside for 5–10 minutes to thicken. Stir again before use.

Place the flour, ground almonds, coconut sugar, coconut, baking powder and salt in a mixing bowl and stir to combine.

Warm the coconut oil in a small saucepan over a low heat until only just melted. Remove from the heat and add the maple syrup, milk, vanilla and the flaxseed mixture. Stir gently with a whisk until well combined. Pour into the dry ingredients and stir until the mixture comes together.

To make the topping, combine ½ cup of the base mixture with the walnuts or almonds in a separate bowl.

Use clean, damp fingers to press the remaining base mixture into the prepared tin in a nice even layer.

Bake for 20 minutes, then allow to cool to room temperature.

To make the filling, place the drained apricots in a food processor or blender and pulse until you have a mixture of finely chopped mince-like pieces and slightly chunkier pieces. The different textures are nice. (Alternatively, mince half the apricots by hand with a knife, and chop the rest a little bit chunkier.)

Transfer the chopped apricots to a medium saucepan. Add the jam, rice syrup, cornflour slurry, vanilla, lemon juice and a pinch of salt and simmer over a medium heat for about 10 minutes, stirring constantly so it doesn't stick and burn. It should end up thick and shiny. Remove from the heat and set aside to cool. To speed it up, you can spread the mixture out on a dinner plate and put it by a window or in the fridge.

When the filling has cooled, scrape it over the baked base and smooth out into an even layer. Sprinkle the nut topping over the apricot filling and gently press it down a little with your fingertips.

Return the tin to the oven and bake for another 17 minutes. The crumb topping should be a golden colour.

Allow to cool to room temperature, then cover and refrigerate for 6–8 hours (or ideally overnight). Cut into squares with a sharp, serrated knife. It will keep for a week in an airtight container in the fridge.

# BANANA BLUEBERRY MUFFINS

**PREP** 15 minutes
**COOK** 30 minutes
**MAKES** 12

- 1 tbsp ground flaxseed
- 5 tbsp cold water
- 2 large ripe bananas
- 1 cup plant-based milk, plus more if needed
- ¾ cup neutral oil or melted coconut oil
- ¼ cup maple syrup
- 1 tbsp pure vanilla extract
- 1 tbsp apple cider vinegar
- 2 cups flour (see tips for gluten-free)
- ¼ cup chickpea flour
- ¾ cup coconut sugar
- ½ cup desiccated coconut
- ¼ cup hemp seeds (optional)
- 1½ tsp ground cinnamon
- 1 tsp baking powder
- 1 tsp baking soda
- ½ tsp salt
- ¾ cup frozen blueberries or sugar-free, plant-based chocolate chips or chopped chocolate

These muffins are on heavy rotation in my kitchen, so much so that I pretty much know the recipe by heart. Obviously they taste good, but also the texture is spot-on (I am particular about this). They're great for lunchboxes and kids love them, but they also have quite a 'grown-up' muffin vibe, so they work for adults, too. And most importantly, they're one of the only things I could cope with toddler Sky 'helping' me with in the kitchen, because you can kind of just do it all in one bowl (or close enough), stir it and you're done. If banana choc chip muffins are a bit more you, sub out the blueberries for chocolate chips or chopped chocolate. I've used frozen wild blueberries for these, and they tend to make the mixture a bit more swirly with blue.

Preheat the oven to 190°C (375°F) regular bake and line a 12-hole muffin tin with paper cases.

Stir the flaxseed and water together in a mug or small bowl and set aside for 5–10 minutes to thicken. Stir again before use.

Mash the bananas in a medium mixing bowl. Add the milk, oil, maple syrup, vanilla, vinegar and flaxseed mixture and stir to combine.

Place the flours, sugar, coconut, hemp (if using), cinnamon, baking powder, baking soda and salt in a larger mixing bowl and whisk to combine. Add the banana mixture and stir until evenly combined.

Stir in the blueberries or chocolate.

Use a ⅓ cup measuring cup to fill the paper cases right to the top (a little bit piled up is even better).

Bake for 25–30 minutes until golden all over (you might need to turn the tray around halfway so they cook evenly). Allow to cool in the tin for about 10 minutes, then transfer to a wire rack to cool. Once cooled completely, store at room temperature in an airtight container. They're lovely warmed up just a smidge the next day with a smear of butter.

### TIPS & SWAPS

- If you use my gluten-free flour blend (see page 222), you may need an extra ¼ cup milk. For store-bought blends, add ⅛ tsp xanthan gum (see page 227).
- Sub out the flaxseed mixture for 1 large lightly beaten free-range egg if you like.

# WHOLE ORANGE & ALMOND CAKE

**PREP** 50 minutes
**COOK** 40 minutes
**MAKES** one medium cake

- 1 whole large (250g / 9 oz) orange
- ⅓ cup water
- 2½ cups ground almonds
- ¾ cup coconut sugar
- ½ cup + 1 tbsp potato starch or cornflour
- 2 tbsp maple syrup or agave syrup
- 3½ tsp baking powder
- 2 tsp pure vanilla extract
- ½ tsp salt

**SYRUP**

- zest of 1 orange
- ¼ cup orange juice
- ¼ cup rice syrup
- 1 tsp pure vanilla extract

The thing I love most about this cake is the whole orange in it, rind and all – the flavour of which only intensifies after it's been baked. The second thing I love is that you simply whizz the ingredients in a food processor and that's the cake batter done – that's my kind of recipe! Ah, the beauty of gluten-free baking. It's not light and fluffy like a regular cake, and it won't rise in the oven. It's slightly more dense, nearly fudgy. The orange syrup at the end elevates it (I prefer to add it just before serving). Don't feel obliged to make the orange slices (I usually don't) – but if you want that extra wow factor, like I did for the recipe shot, then it's a nice option (see tip). Serve with a dollop of coconut yoghurt.

First, simmer the orange to reduce the bitterness. Add the whole orange, skin and all, to a medium saucepan filled with water and simmer it for about 30 minutes. Remove from the saucepan and leave until cool enough to handle.

Preheat the oven to 170°C (325°F) regular bake and line the base and sides of a 20–21cm (8–8¼ in) round springform cake tin with baking paper.

Roughly chop the orange, discarding any seeds. Place it in a food processor along with the water and whizz until you have a smooth smush, scraping down the sides as you go. A few small bits of rind is fine.

Add the ground almonds, coconut sugar, potato starch or cornflour, maple or agave syrup, baking powder, vanilla and salt to the food processor. Whizz again a few times briefly, scraping the sides, until you have a smooth batter.

Spoon the batter into the prepared tin and smooth it out as nicely as you can with a spoon or a spatula. The cake doesn't rise or smooth out in the oven, so you have to do it prior to baking unless you want a bumpy cake!

Bake for about 40 minutes, or until a skewer inserted into the centre comes out mostly clean (a few crumbs are okay). Leave to cool in the tin.

To make the syrup, combine the ingredients in a small saucepan. Add a pinch of salt and simmer over a medium heat for a few minutes until reduced by half. Leave to cool to room temperature. If it cools down too sticky, reheat with more juice or water until it's the right consistency.

Pour the syrup over the whole cake before slicing, or over the individual slices when serving.

## TIPS & SWAPS

- I like using organic oranges for this cake since all the skin goes in. You need about 250g (9 oz) in total, so use 2 oranges if necessary and halve one once they're cooked.
- To make the sliced orange topping seen in the photo, cut an orange into 5mm (¼ in) slices. Place in a saucepan with ½ cup rice syrup and ½ cup water and simmer over a low heat for a few minutes. Transfer the slices to a baking tray lined with baking paper and dry in the oven at 70°C (150°F) regular bake for a few hours, until tacky and soft. While the slices are cooking, keep basting them with the rice syrup mixture so they stay sticky and gooey. Any remaining rice syrup mixture can be drizzled over the slices at the end, before you arrange them on top of the cake.

# THE CHOCOLATE MONSTER

**PREP** 15 minutes
**COOK** 1 hour
**MAKES** 1 medium cake

- 1½ cups flour (see tips for gluten-free)
- 1¼ cups coconut sugar
- ½ cup dark cocoa powder
- 1 tsp baking soda
- ¾ tsp salt
- 1½ cups cold water
- ½ cup grapeseed or rice bran oil
- ¼ cup maple syrup
- 1 tbsp balsamic vinegar
- 1 tbsp pure vanilla extract

**ICING**

- 300g (10½ oz) pitted dates
- ⅓ cup maple syrup
- 200g (7 oz) butter (plant-based or regular)
- ¼ cup dark cocoa powder
- 2 tsp pure vanilla extract or paste
- ½ tsp salt

**TO DECORATE (OPTIONAL)**

- finely chopped chocolate (sugar-free and plant-based if preferred)

My Crazy Italian Chocolate Cake is already a solid staple in kitchens across the country. So what's this new one about? Well, I wanted to create a version for my boys without refined sugar (let's not forget the icing on the original is made with an entire large block of chocolate). So look, while I'm not a great fan of just shoving dates in everything (it's been done), in this chocolate 'buttercream' icing the way they behave after being whipped up is nothing short of a miracle. I can't remember the last time I made chocolate cake or icing any other way, because it's so good, and so very easy. You could even slice the cake horizontally and add a layer of icing for extra height and wow factor. Make sure you use a smallish tin as specified, or it will look flat.

Preheat the oven to 160°C (315°F) regular bake and line the base and sides of a 20–22cm (8–8½ in) round cake tin with baking paper.

Place the flour, coconut sugar, cocoa, baking soda and salt in a medium-large mixing bowl and stir with a whisk to combine to a fine powder with no lumps.

Make a well in the centre and add the water, oil, maple syrup, vinegar and vanilla. Stir gently with the whisk until smooth and combined.

Scrape the mixture into the prepared tin with a spatula and bake for 1 hour, or until a skewer inserted into the centre comes out clean. Leave to cool in the tin for about 10 minutes, then transfer to a wire rack to cool. Ice when the cake is completely cool.

To make the icing, soak the dates in a bowl of just-boiled water for 10 minutes (set a timer). Drain well, then transfer to a food processor along with the maple syrup. Process until very smooth — you will probably have to scrape the sides down quite a few times before the mixture catches and smooths out properly. Place in the fridge to cool right down.

When you're ready to ice the cake, add the remaining ingredients to the food processor with the chilled date paste and whizz until smooth.

Spread onto the cooled cake. If the icing seems too soft, just refrigerate it until it firms up a bit. Top with the chopped chocolate (if using) just before serving.

### TIPS & SWAPS

- If using store-bought gluten-free flour blend, add ⅛ tsp xanthan gum to the mixture.
- If using my homemade gluten-free flour blend (see page 222), use 1¾ cups water and no extra xanthan gum.

# CHRISTMAS CAKE

**PREP** 40 minutes, plus 6+ hours soaking time

**COOK** 3 hours 30 minutes

**MAKES** 1 medium cake

- 800g (1 lb 12 oz) dried fruit, chopped (raisins, sultanas, figs, apricots, glacé cherries, dates)
- 75g (2½ oz) mixed peel or finely chopped zest of 2 oranges
- 400ml (14 fl oz) hot chai or regular tea
- 100ml (3½ fl oz) brandy, sherry, port, whiskey or rum
- 1 large banana (yellow but not too spotty)
- 3 tbsp ground flaxseed
- ¾ cup muscovado sugar or 1 cup coconut sugar
- ½ cup semi-solid coconut oil
- ⅓ cup almond or cashew butter
- 2 tsp pure vanilla extract or paste
- ½ cup buckwheat flour
- ½ cup brown or white rice flour
- ½ cup cornflour
- ¼ cup ground almonds
- 2 tbsp cocoa powder
- 1 tsp baking powder
- 1 tsp baking soda
- 1 tsp psyllium husk
- 1½ tsp mixed spice
- 1½ tsp ground cinnamon
- 1½ tsp ground ginger
- ½ tsp ground nutmeg
- ¼ tsp ground cloves
- ½ tsp salt

**TO DECORATE (CHOOSE SOME OR ALL)**

- ¼ cup brandy, sherry, port, whiskey or rum, for pouring
- warmed sugar-free apricot jam, golden syrup or rice syrup
- whole roasted almonds, pecans, walnuts, hazelnuts or macadamias
- sliced crystallised ginger, glacé cherries or extra dried fruit or mixed peel
- gold foil, gold pearls or edible glitter

Christmas cake is something that's grown on me considerably as I've 'matured'. There are so many things I can appreciate about it now, whereas when I was young all I cared about was chocolate and candy canes. Done right, there's something very special about a cake like this, and now the festive season doesn't feel complete without it! Considering traditionally these cakes are built on a foundation of eggs, dairy and gluten, I have a feeling this recipe might be quite exciting for many of you who've been struggling to find something that tastes and feels like the real deal. And excited you should be; no one would ever know it's made without the usual suspects because it's very rich, spicy, fruity, fudgy and decadent. The alcohol will cook off in the oven, but you can replace it with extra tea. You can also double this recipe for a huge cake.

Combine the dried fruit and peel or zest in a large mixing bowl. Pour the hot chai or tea and the alcohol over the top and stir to combine. Squish the fruit down under the liquid, cover and leave for a minimum of 6 hours – or up to a week.

When ready to cook, place the fruit in a sieve sitting over a bowl and allow to drain for 5 minutes, reserving the soaking liquid.

Preheat the oven to 150°C (300°F) regular bake.

Line a 21cm (8¼ in) square slice tin or 22cm (8½ in) round cake tin with paper. If you're using a regular tin, line it with a couple of sheets of newspaper or brown paper (try supermarket paper bags) first, then with baking paper (no gaps!). If you're using a wooden cake box, you only need to line it with baking paper.

Mash the banana well. Mash the flaxseed in well and leave for 10 minutes.

Place the sugar and coconut oil in a mixing bowl and beat with an electric beater for a few minutes until creamy. Add the banana mixture, almond or cashew butter and vanilla and beat again. Set aside.

Place the flours, ground almonds, cocoa, baking powder, baking soda, psyllium husk, spices and salt in your largest mixing bowl and stir to combine. Add the dried fruit and stir so all the fruit is coated with the flour mixture.

Add the banana mixture to the fruit mixture, along with ½ cup of the reserved fruit soaking liquid. Fold to combine evenly. Transfer to the prepared tin and smooth it out evenly so it fills all the corners.

Bake for 1 hour, then turn down the oven to 120°C (235°F) and bake for a further 2 hours 30 minutes. A skewer inserted into the centre should come out clean.

If you like, you can tip an extra ¼ cup of alcohol over the top as soon as it comes out of the oven. Leave to cool completely in the tin. The undecorated cake will keep for weeks in an airtight container in a cool, dry place. If you are somewhere warm, store it in the fridge. The outer pieces will have a cakey texture, while the inside will be fudgier.

A day or so before serving, brush the cake generously with a thick layer of jam or syrup, then press nuts and dried fruits of your choice lightly into the top. Brush with more glaze to finish. For a truly magical, festive feel, adorn the top and sides with gold foil, pearls or glitter.

For an optional booze injection, make skewer holes in the cake after a week or so and drizzle a little extra alcohol in. This helps preserve the cake as well as adding 'oomph' and moisture. The cake will keep for many weeks if you do this.

# GLUTEN-FREE FRUIT TOAST

**PREP** 30 minutes, plus 1 hour 45 minutes rising time

**COOK** 45 minutes

**MAKES** 1 medium loaf

### BOOSTER

- 1 cup gluten-free flour blend (see page 222)
- ½ cup buckwheat flour
- 2 tbsp coconut sugar
- 2 tsp active yeast granules (check expiry date)
- 2 cups water

### DOUGH

- 1¼ cups tapioca flour
- ¼ cup chickpea flour
- ½ cup ground almonds
- 3 tbsp coconut sugar
- 2 tbsp psyllium husk
- 2 tbsp ground flaxseed
- 1 tbsp mixed spice
- 1 tbsp ground cinnamon
- 1½ tsp ground ginger
- ¾ tsp ground cloves
- 2½ tsp baking powder
- 1 tsp xanthan gum
- 1 tsp salt
- ¼ cup grapeseed or sunflower oil
- 1 tsp apple cider vinegar
- 1½ cups raisins, sultanas and/or currants
- zest of 2 oranges (see tip)

### TO SERVE (OPTIONAL)

- plant-based butter
- sugar-free jam, honey or marmalade

Look at the state of it — who doesn't want to bite into that?! Warm, toasty aromatic spices, juicy pieces of fruit, lashings of whatever butter you choose, a meltingly delicious and nostalgic crunch with every bite. This whole thing kicked off with me aiming for gluten-free hot cross buns. At some point in the process, I realised they were always destined to be a loaf. And what a loaf! Although it took me many, many iterations to get it right, it's a complete doddle to make. I have a feeling you'll be surprised and yes, even delighted. And because there's no gluten, there's no kneading required. Heck, you don't need to be gluten-free to enjoy it, because anyone who's a fruit toast fiend is gonna delight in this. Then at Easter time, just pipe a cross on top before baking and you're sorted.

Line a medium loaf tin with baking paper all the way up the sides.

To make the booster, place the ingredients in a medium-large mixing bowl and whisk to combine. Cover with a clean, damp tea towel and leave in a draught-free place for about 45 minutes (a turned-off oven with a mug of just-boiled water or the hot water cupboard works nicely). After 45 minutes it should be starting to puff/bubble up nicely.

While the booster is working, get the dry ingredients for the dough ready. Combine the flours, ground almonds, coconut sugar, psyllium husk, flaxseed, spices, baking powder, xanthan gum and salt in the bowl of a stand mixer with a paddle attachment (or a large, deep mixing bowl).

When the booster is ready, add it to the dry ingredients along with the oil and vinegar. Turn the mixer to medium-high and beat for 4 minutes, or if using a bowl, beat for 2–3 minutes using a handheld electric beater on medium speed.

Add the dried fruit and orange zest and mix again on a very slow speed to only just combine.

Scrape the mixture (it will be a thick batter) into the prepared loaf tin using a spatula, smooth out the top and leave to sit for about an hour in the turned-off oven. The loaf should nearly double in size after an hour or so — it may take a little more time or a little less, but this is okay. It will finish rising a tiny bit when baked because of the baking powder.

Preheat the oven to 200°C (400°F) regular bake (take the loaf out first!).

Bake the loaf for 35 minutes. Remove from the oven, allow to cool for 10 minutes in the tin, then transfer to a wire rack.

Once cool, cut into slices with a bread knife. It keeps for a few days in a sealed container at room temperature, or longer in the fridge.

Now the crucial part — TOAST IT! That's when the flavours really come out. Then slather with butter and jam, honey or marmalade.

### TIPS & SWAPS

- I thinly peel the rind off my oranges with a peeler, then finely chop it, so I get more intense orange bits.
- For a nut-free version, use finely whizzed up sunflower seeds in place of the ground almonds.

# BOUNTY SLICE

**PREP** 20 minutes, plus 3+ hours setting time

**MAKES** about 20 pieces

### FILLING

6 cups desiccated coconut

½ cup thick coconut cream

½ cup rice syrup

⅓ cup maple syrup or agave syrup

⅓ cup melted coconut oil

1 tbsp pure vanilla extract or paste

1 tsp salt

### COATING

½ cup + 2 tbsp coconut oil

½ cup + 2 tbsp maple syrup or agave syrup

½ cup dark cocoa powder

Ah, the sweet simplicity of these two heroic flavours, chocolate and coconut, bravely leading the charge on my tastebuds like Aragorn storming the orc army (even though he was horribly outnumbered). Nothing else is needed except a wee smidge of vanilla. This recipe is so easy to whip up when you need to take a sweet somewhere — another highly convenient situation whereby everything gets shoved unceremoniously into a food processor and whizzed into creation. The stovetop chocolate is lush and I do love to slurp a little bit when it's still melted, if I'm being honest.

Line the base and sides of a 20cm (8 in) square slice tin with baking paper.

To make the filling, place the ingredients in a food processor and whizz until combined. You'll need to scrape down the sides to make sure it's all incorporated.

Tip the mixture into the prepared tin and press down hard into an even layer. Use the back of a dessertspoon to get it smooth and clean up the edges at the end. Really pack it in there so it doesn't crumble later. Cover and freeze for a few hours until it's very firm.

To make the coating, place the coconut oil and maple or agave syrup in a heatproof bowl sitting over a saucepan of simmering water. When melted, remove the bowl from the heat and whisk to combine. Add the cocoa and a pinch of salt and stir with the whisk until smooth.

Pour the coating over the chilled base and refrigerate for at least an hour until set.

When set, cut into bars with a sharp knife and store in an airtight container. They will last in the fridge for a couple of weeks or in the freezer for up to a month.

# BANANA LOAF

**PREP** 15 minutes
**COOK** 1 hour 10 minutes
**MAKES** 1 medium loaf

1 tbsp ground flaxseed
3 tbsp cold water
2 large ripe bananas
¾ cup plant-based milk
½ cup neutral oil, such as grapeseed or sunflower
1 cup coconut sugar
¼ cup maple syrup
2 tbsp lemon juice or apple cider vinegar
1 tbsp pure vanilla extract or paste
2 cups flour (see tips for gluten-free)
1½ tsp ground cinnamon
1 tsp baking soda
¾ tsp baking powder
½ tsp salt

**As I was testing this recipe, I wondered if a plain banana loaf was too humdrum to include — I mean, there's no fancy yoghurt, coconut, nuts, berries, flakes, LSA, oats or anything here. No la-di-da. Just a hint of cinnamon. Then I suddenly realised this was what made the loaf special. It's an honest, simple ode to ripe bananas. Sometimes classic and pared back is refreshing.**

Preheat the oven to 160°C (315°F) regular bake and line the base and sides of a medium loaf tin with baking paper.

Stir the flaxseed and water together in a mug or small bowl and set aside for 5–10 minutes to thicken. Stir again before use.

Mash the bananas in a large mixing bowl. Add the milk, oil, coconut sugar, maple syrup, lemon juice or vinegar and vanilla to the bowl. Add the flaxseed mixture and whisk gently to combine.

Place the flour, cinnamon, baking soda, baking powder and salt in another bowl and stir with a whisk to combine. Add to the banana mixture and fold to combine evenly.

Pour into the prepared tin and bake for 1 hour 10 minutes, or until a skewer comes out clean.

Allow to cool on a wire rack. It will be tricky to slice warm (but easiest using a serrated knife if you must). Personally, I find it nicer the next day when the flavours have intensified and it's even more cakey.

Once completely cooled, store in an airtight container at room temperature or in the fridge.

## TIPS & SWAPS

- You can use my gluten-free flour blend (see page 222) or a store-bought gluten-free flour blend instead of plain flour. If you use a store-bought one, add ⅛ tsp xanthan gum to the dry mix too. (My blend is going to turn out way nicer, FYI.)
- If your bananas aren't very ripe and spotty, this loaf won't taste as flavoursome.
- If you happen to be using canned chickpeas for something, try saving 7 tbsp of the liquid from the can (aquafaba) and use an electric beater to whip it up in a clean bowl until soft peaks form. Fold this through the loaf batter at the end just before baking — and omit the flaxseed mixture altogether. It makes for a slightly lighter loaf, but both versions are good.

# IRON BOOST BARS

**PREP** 20 minutes, plus 3+ hours setting time

**COOK** 15 minutes

**MAKES** about 35 small bars

- 500g (1 lb 2 oz) dried apricots, chopped finely
- ½ cup chopped dates
- ¾ cup rice syrup
- ⅓ cup coconut oil
- 1 tsp pure vanilla extract
- 1½ cups pumpkin seeds
- ¾ cup sunflower seeds
- ½ cup buckwheat groats
- 1 cup puffed rice cereal (gluten-free if preferred)
- ½ cup desiccated coconut
- ½ cup chia seeds
- ¼ tsp salt
- ¾ cup chocolate chips or chopped chocolate (optional but yum; sugar-free and plant-based if preferred)

When I was pregnant with Sage, my iron levels weren't even close to what they should be, and I was determined to remedy that as much as I could through diet (since that's kinda my thing). I did lots of research and came to the happy realisation that there were a bunch of naturally iron-rich foods that would combine perfectly into a heavenly muesli bar! So I had a play and this recipe came together amazingly easily. Lordy it's good – I'm not sure if it was what helped in the end, but I sure enjoyed eating it. As well as being fuel for anyone who loves a tasty yet nourishing snack (not just preggers ladies and new mums), these bars are a perfect addition to school lunchboxes as they're nut-free, gluten-free and of course, refined-sugar-free (if you use the right chocolate).

Line the base and sides of a 20cm (8 in) square slice tin with baking paper.

Place the chopped apricots, dates, rice syrup, coconut oil and vanilla in a medium saucepan over a medium-low heat. Stir often with a wooden spoon as it all starts to melt and soften – give it a good 10 minutes until it's mushy. Set aside.

Whizz half the pumpkin and sunflower seeds in a food processor until you have a coarse crumb with some larger seed pieces. Leave the other half of the seeds whole.

Dry-toast the buckwheat groats in a small pan over a medium-high heat, shaking the pan every now and then, for a couple of minutes until they start to pop. This step makes them crunchier.

Place the chopped seeds, whole seeds, toasted buckwheat, puffed rice, coconut, chia and salt in a large mixing bowl and stir to combine.

Add the warm apricot mixture and stir with a strong wooden spoon until combined.

Scatter the chocolate (if using) over the base of the prepared tin. Scrape the warm slice mixture on top and squash it down as firmly as you can using clean, wet hands. Use the back of a dessertspoon to smooth and flatten the top. If it's compacted, it will hold together better and be easier to cut.

Cover and refrigerate for at least 3 hours until chilled, then cut into small squares with a sharp knife.

Store in an airtight container. It will last in the fridge for a few weeks or in the freezer for a few months.

### TIPS & SWAPS

- I like to use sulphur-free dried apricots when I can find them. Way better for ya.

# GINGERBREAD LOAF

**PREP** 20 minutes
**COOK** 1 hour 10 minutes
**MAKES** 1 medium loaf

- 1 cup coconut sugar
- ¾ cup milk (plant-based or regular)
- ½ cup grapeseed or sunflower oil
- ⅓ cup molasses (or maple syrup)
- 2 tbsp finely grated fresh ginger
- 2 tsp pure vanilla extract or paste
- 2 cups flour (see tips for gluten-free)
- 2 tsp ground cinnamon
- 1½ tsp ground ginger
- 1 tsp baking soda
- ½ tsp salt
- 6 tbsp aquafaba (the liquid from canned chickpeas)

**TO SERVE (OPTIONAL)**

- butter (plant-based or regular)

This recipe makes a moist, rich-tasting, gingery loaf. The good dollop of molasses in there is very traditional, and adds a subtle sweet depth (like a slightly smoky, burnt caramel vibe) which pairs perfectly with those warm spices – see if you can pick up on it. You should be able to find it at your supermarket but you can use maple syrup at a pinch.

Preheat the oven to 160°C (315°F) regular bake and line a medium loaf tin with baking paper so it goes up and over the sides.

Place the coconut sugar, milk, oil, molasses or maple syrup, grated ginger and vanilla in a medium bowl and whisk gently until evenly combined.

Sift the flour, cinnamon, ground ginger, baking soda and salt into a large mixing bowl and stir together.

Make a well in the centre of the dry ingredients and add the wet ingredients. Stir with a whisk until evenly combined.

Place the aquafaba in a small, clean mixing bowl and whisk until no liquid remains – it doesn't have to form firm peaks. Stir evenly into the loaf batter.

Pour the batter into the prepared tin and bake for 1 hour 10 minutes, or until a skewer inserted into the centre comes out clean.

Let it stand in the tin for 10 minutes, then transfer to a wire rack to cool. If you can't wait until it's completely cool before digging in, it will be a little messy to cut.

It will last in an airtight container at room temperature for a couple of days, or in the fridge for longer. I think it's nicer on day two, and certainly easier to slice. Serve with a smear of plant-based butter and a nice chai latte.

### TIPS & SWAPS

- To make this gluten-free, either use my gluten-free flour blend (see page 222) or use store-bought gluten-free flour plus an added ¼ tsp xanthan gum.
- If you don't have aquafaba, you can soak 1 tbsp ground flaxseed in 3 tbsp water, then add it to the mixture – the result is slightly more dense, but still lovely. Or you can use the liquid from canned cannellini beans instead of chickpeas.
- If you don't have fresh ginger, bump up the ground ginger to 1½ tbsp.

# LEMON CREAM PIE

**PREP** 40 minutes, plus 6+ hours setting time

**COOK** 15 minutes

**SERVES** 6

**BASE**

- ½ cup ground almonds
- ½ cup brown rice flour
- ½ cup buckwheat flour
- 2 tbsp tapioca flour, arrowroot flour or cornflour
- ⅓ cup coconut sugar
- 2 tsp psyllium husk
- ½ cup coconut oil, melted but not hot
- 2 tbsp just-boiled water
- 1 tsp pure vanilla extract

**FILLING**

- 2 cups full-fat coconut cream (I use the Kara brand in a carton)
- ½ cup + 1 tbsp agave syrup or maple syrup
- 3 tbsp coconut oil
- 3 tbsp plant-based butter
- 3 tbsp lemon zest
- ½ cup lemon juice
- ¼ tsp ground turmeric
- ¼ tsp salt
- ¼ cup cornflour mixed with ¼ cup plant-based milk to make a slurry

**TO SERVE (OPTIONAL)**

- fresh berries, such as raspberries, blueberries or sliced strawberries
- edible flowers
- whipped cream (plant-based if preferred)

If you're a lemon fan (and honestly, who isn't?), you're gonna want to try this because I have not held back on the zesty citrus injection. It's such a refreshingly easy recipe to make – I especially love the crust part because there's no precarious rolling, flipping or transferring of pastry and no faffing with baking beads or sagging during cooking – just smoodge the base evenly into the tin, bake naked (the tart, not you), cool, then add the cooked lemon filling (also a cinch to make). It's a little rustic yet still very elegant, and it tastes utterly divine. I've made the crust gluten-free (which I recommend as it's so crispy), but you can also use plain flour (see tip).

Preheat the oven to 180°C (350°F) regular bake and have a 23cm (9 in) round pie tin, tart tin or springform cake tin ready.

To make the base, combine the ground almonds, flours, sugar, psyllium husk and a pinch of salt in a medium mixing bowl. Make a well in the centre and add the coconut oil, hot water and vanilla. Stir until the mixture just comes together.

While it's still warm, crumble two-thirds of the mixture around the edges of the tin (the sides of the crust will be a little thicker than the base) and press it 3–4cm (1¼–1½ in) up the sides of the tin (you can use the back of a dessertspoon for this). You want the edges to be an even thickness.

Crumble the remaining dough over the base and press it down into an even, smooth layer (you can use the back of the spoon or the base of a metal measuring cup for this). It should end up about 5mm (¼ in) thick. Take care that it's not too thick where the base meets the sides, or it ends up like a massive wedge. Lightly press down any jagged ridges on the sides with a finger.

Bake for 15 minutes, then remove from the oven and allow to cool completely before filling.

To make the filling, place the coconut cream, agave or maple syrup, oil, butter, lemon zest and juice, turmeric and salt in a medium saucepan. Stir in the cornflour slurry. Place over a medium heat and stir constantly with a whisk until thickened – it might take a while, then suddenly start thickening, so don't leave it alone. It should start to bubble a bit and be the consistency of thick, shiny custard.

Remove from the heat, transfer to a mixing bowl and to allow to cool – don't refrigerate it. If you like, you can lay a piece of clingfilm on the surface to stop a skin forming.

When the filling is lukewarm, whisk it quickly to smooth out any lumps, then scrape it into the baked crust. Cover and refrigerate for at least 6 hours to set properly – leave it overnight if you can.

When ready to serve, scatter the top with berries and edible flowers (if using) and serve with whipped cream on the side if desired.

Leftovers can be stored in an airtight container in the fridge for a day or two.

### TIPS & SWAPS

- Dairy-free whipping cream is now available at all good supermarkets.
- If you're not eating gluten-free, you can use 1 cup plain flour in place of the flours. Cook the base for 20 minutes.

# STICKY DATE PUDDING

**PREP** 15 minutes
**COOK** 1 hour
**SERVES** 4–6

### PUDDING

- 2 tbsp ground flaxseed mixed with 6 tbsp cold water
- 400g (14 oz) pitted dates, roughly chopped
- 1 cup water
- ½ cup coconut oil
- ½ cup coconut cream
- ¼ cup coconut sugar
- 2 tbsp maple syrup, honey or coconut nectar
- 2 tsp pure vanilla extract
- zest of 1 large orange
- 1 tsp baking soda
- 1 cup flour or gluten-free flour blend (see page 222 or use store-bought)
- 2 tsp ground cinnamon
- ½ tsp salt

### SAUCE

- 2 x 400g (14 oz) cans full-fat coconut cream
- ¾ cup coconut sugar
- 1 tbsp pure vanilla extract

### TO SERVE (OPTIONAL)

- ice cream (plant-based if preferred)

There's something so inherently good about a sticky date pudding (I mean, for one, it's called Sticky Date Pudding). And yes, as a naked pudding it's a terribly unglamorous sight being pulled from the oven, but once it's spooned steaming into a serving bowl, nestled in beside a seductively melting scoop of ice cream and liberally smothered in rich, fudgy butterscotch sauce — well, will you just look at it? I'm so in love with this photo because it encapsulates everything I love about this splendidly old-fashioned (maybe slightly underrated?) dessert. It couldn't be simpler to put together and dang, I wish I'd known how easy it was to create a simple yet epic dairy-free butterscotch sauce before now!

Preheat the oven to 160°C (315°F) regular bake and grease a 20–25cm (8–10 in) oven dish.

To make the pudding, mix the flaxseed with the water and set aside. Place the dates, water, coconut oil, coconut cream, coconut sugar, maple syrup, honey or coconut nectar, vanilla and orange zest in a saucepan over a medium-high heat. Bring to the boil then let it bubble away for about 3 minutes. Remove from the heat.

Give the flaxseed mixture a stir. Add the baking soda to the hot date mixture and stir with a wooden spoon to combine. Add the flour, flaxseed mixture, cinnamon and salt and stir again to combine.

Pour into the prepared dish and bake for 1 hour.

To make the butterscotch sauce, place the ingredients in a saucepan over a medium-low heat. Add a pinch of salt and simmer until reduced by about half (it might take a while). Pour a third of the sauce over the pudding in the last 5 minutes of baking, then transfer the rest to a jug for serving.

Serve the pudding hot, topped with the butterscotch sauce and accompanied by your favourite ice cream.

### TIPS & SWAPS

- You can use 2 lightly beaten free-range eggs in place of the flaxseed mixture if you like.

# GOLDEN PUMPKIN PIE

**PREP** 1 hour, plus 6+ hours setting time

**COOK** 1 hour

**SERVES** 8

**FILLING**

1.8–2kg (4 lb–4 lb 8 oz) pumpkin, skin-on

1⅓ cups coconut cream (I use the Kara brand in a carton)

⅓ cup maple syrup or agave syrup

¼ cup coconut sugar

¼ cup + 1 tsp cornflour

¼ cup melted coconut oil

1 tbsp pure vanilla extract

2 tsp ground cinnamon

2 tsp ground ginger

1 tsp ground nutmeg

½ tsp mixed spice

¼ tsp ground cloves

¾ tsp salt

**CRUST**

1½ cups flour or gluten-free flour blend (see page 222)

½ cup walnuts

¼ cup coconut sugar

¼ tsp salt

150g (5½ oz) solid coconut oil

1–2 tbsp ice-cold water

**TO SERVE (OPTIONAL)**

handful of walnut halves

maple syrup

TIPS & SWAPS

- You can use any variety of pumpkin; butternut squash is also good. I've even replaced half the pumpkin with orange kūmara and it was delicious! If you don't have fresh pumpkin you can use 2 cups pumpkin purée instead and skip the roasting step.
- To make this gluten-free, either use my gluten-free flour blend (see page 222) or use store-bought gluten-free flour plus 1 tsp xanthan gum.
- Pop the coconut oil in the freezer for 5–10 minutes if it's soft.

The original pumpkin pie in *Homemade Happiness* was such a resounding success, it was a no-brainer for me to include a plant-based version here (also the pumpkins here in Taranaki are outstanding – golden and flavoursome, so I'm constantly inspired). As fate would have it, a good friend from the States was visiting me recently. She's eaten pumpkin pie just about every year of her life and after tasting this one (and becoming slightly emotional), remarked it was one of the best, if not the best, she'd tasted. She said it was well balanced – texture, flavour, sweetness, spice, mouthfeel, and it reminded her of her childhood. Isn't that just divine? So don't just take my word for it! I find it better to make this the night before you want to eat it, so the flavours have time to develop.

Preheat the oven to 180°C (350°F) regular bake and have a 23cm (9 in) round pie tin, tart tin or springform cake tin ready.

Remove the seeds from the pumpkin. Cut the flesh into large pieces, skin on, and place in a large baking dish with ¾ cup water to cover the bottom of the dish. Cover with foil and bake for 45–60 minutes, or until the pumpkin is soft. You can add a little more water if needed. Remove from the oven, leaving the oven on, and allow to cool.

When it's cool enough to handle, discard the skin and whizz the flesh in a food processor until smooth. A handheld blender and tall jug would also work well here. Measure out 2 cups of pumpkin purée to use in the pie – any spare purée can be used in soup, muffins or smoothies, fed to a baby or frozen.

To make the crust, give the food processor a quick wash. Add the flour, walnuts, coconut sugar and salt and pulse until you have a coarse crumb. Add the coconut oil and 1 tbsp cold water, and pulse until you have a sticky crumb that's just starting to come together into a dough (add a little more water if necessary).

Crumble two-thirds of the dough around the edges of the tin (the sides of the crust will be a little thicker than the base). Press the dough about 5cm (2 in) up the sides of the tin. You want the dough around the edge to be of even thickness.

Crumble the remaining dough over the base and press it into an even layer about 5mm (¼ in) thick. You can use the back of a dessertspoon or the base of a metal measuring cup to flatten it out. Take care that it's not too thick where the base meets the sides, or it ends up like a massive wedge. Lightly press down any jagged ridges on the sides with a finger.

Bake for 15 minutes. Remove from the oven, leaving the oven on, and allow to cool before filling.

To make the filling, give the food processor another quick clean and add the pumpkin purée, along with all the remaining filling ingredients. Whizz until silky smooth. (Or you can whisk it in a bowl by hand if you prefer.) Pour the filling into the crust and give the top a quick once-over with a spatula to smooth it out.

Bake in the 180°C (350°F) oven for an hour, or until it feels firmish in the centre.

Leave the cooked pie to cool completely, then cover tightly and refrigerate for at least 6 hours. The longer you can wait to dig in, the better it tastes, even a couple of days later! Serve warm or cold.

If making the optional topping, simmer the walnuts and maple syrup in a pan until the syrup thickens. Set aside to cool, then scatter over the pie.

# BERRIES & CREAM CHEESECAKE

**PREP** 40 minutes, plus 6+ hours setting time
**SERVES** 8

### BASE

8 pitted dates
1½ cups ground almonds
¾ cup desiccated coconut
2 tbsp melted coconut oil
2 tbsp maple syrup
1 tsp pure vanilla extract
¼ tsp salt

### FILLING

720g (1 lb 9½ oz) plant-based cream cheese, chilled
½ cup agave syrup or maple syrup
1½ tbsp vanilla paste or 2 tbsp pure vanilla extract
zest of 1 lemon
1 tbsp lemon juice
1 cup plant-based whipping cream, chilled

### COULIS

2½ cups frozen raspberries
3 tbsp maple syrup or agave syrup

### TO SERVE

1–2 punnets sliced strawberries, or fresh berries of choice

FINALLY! A nut-free, dairy-free cheesecake *without icing sugar* that's simple to make and tastes absolutely outstanding (I've worked very hard to bring this to you, just so you know). Several people have joyfully exclaimed that it's the best cheesecake they've tasted. It's got that real classic feel about it. I feel like this recipe performs at its absolute best in summer, piled with ripe red strawberries – but you can use any berries available throughout the year (blueberries would work). I can't stress enough how important it is to splash out and use vanilla paste for this one so you get that traditional cheesecake flavour happening. Also, make sure you look for a dairy-free cream that whips (some of them don't). Good supermarkets stock it chilled in a carton. You can also sub in regular cream cheese and/or whipped cream, if that's your vibe.

Line the base and sides of a 21–23cm (8¼–9 in) round springform cake tin with baking paper (the smaller your tin, the higher your cheesecake will be).

To make the base, soak the dates in a bowl of very hot water for 5 minutes, then drain. Place in a food processor, add the remaining base ingredients and whizz to a fine crumb. Tip into the prepared tin and press firmly into an even layer (use the back of a dessertspoon to get it smooth and even). Set aside.

To make the filling, place the cream cheese in a mixing bowl (deep sides means fewer splatters). Using a handheld electric beater, beat on low, then increase the speed to high until the cream cheese is smooth and creamy with no lumps. It will be difficult at first, but it will soften up fairly quickly. Scrape the sides so it's all incorporated.

Immediately add 2 tbsp of the agave or maple syrup and beat until only just incorporated. Repeat until the syrup is used up, scraping down the sides as you go. Lastly, beat in the vanilla and lemon zest and juice. Wash and dry the beaters.

Place the whipping cream in a mixing bowl and beat until firmly whipped. Fold ¼ cup of the whipped cream through the cream cheese mixture (it will take a bit of folding at first). Add the remaining whipped cream and fold through to combine evenly.

Scrape the filling on top of the base, smooth out, cover and refrigerate for 6 hours or overnight.

To make the berry coulis, place the raspberries and maple or agave syrup in a small saucepan and simmer for a few minutes until soft and mushy. Strain through a sieve, using a spatula to push through as much liquid as you can. Discard the seeds and mush left in the sieve and set aside the coulis until needed.

To serve, remove the cheesecake from the tin and transfer to a serving plate. Drizzle with the coulis and slice with a hot knife. Top with the fresh berries.

This cheesecake keeps in the fridge for a few days, or can be sealed tightly (without the toppings) and frozen for a couple of weeks.

### TIPS & SWAPS

- You can replace the ground almonds with 150g (5½ oz) plain biscuits that suit your dietary requirements and an extra 1 tbsp each of oil and maple syrup.
- If you can't find dairy-free whipping cream (and you can't use regular cream), use a 400g (14 oz) can full-fat coconut cream, without emulsifiers or stabilisers – chilled in the fridge for 24 hours. Scrape the solid cream part out and beat that before folding it into the cream cheese mixture.

# APPLE & RHUBARB CRUMBLE

**PREP** 25 minutes
**COOK** 45 minutes
**SERVES** 6

**CRUMBLE**

1 cup sunflower seeds
⅓ cup walnuts
½ cup flour or gluten-free flour blend (see page 222)
½ cup ground almonds
½ cup desiccated coconut
½ cup coconut sugar
⅓ cup hemp seeds
½ tsp baking powder
¼ tsp salt
½ cup softened coconut oil
¼ cup rice syrup or maple syrup
1 tsp pure vanilla extract

**FILLING**

6–7 Granny Smith apples, peeled, cored and thinly sliced
400g (14 oz) rhubarb, cut into 1–2cm (½–¾ in) chunks
½ cup maple syrup
¼ cup cornflour or custard powder
¼ cup coconut sugar
1 tbsp lemon juice
1 tbsp pure vanilla extract
2 tsp ground cinnamon
¼ tsp salt

**TO SERVE (OPTIONAL)**

ice cream, coconut yoghurt or chilled coconut cream

I was determined to bring a damn-good crumble recipe into existence without using any oats (seeing as there are so many of you out there who can't have them). I tried out loads of different things in their stead, and it turns out sunflower seeds are the hero we didn't know we needed here. It's unquestionably still a superbly comforting dish — I've taken a classic and revamped it a bit, but it's lost none of the nostalgic magic that makes a good crumble what it is. Like, you could probably serve it to your gran and she'd love it. Lucky you if you have your own rhubarb patch! I've just planted my first homegrown seedlings but they're a while off. Luckily, the store-bought (or gifted) stuff works a treat, too.

Preheat the oven to 170°C (325°F) regular bake and have a shallow medium oven dish ready. (I love enamelware for this.)

To make the crumble, place all the crumble ingredients in a food processor and pulse until you have a very chunky crumb.

To make the filling, combine all the ingredients in a mixing bowl and toss to combine evenly. Tip into the oven dish and press firmly into an even layer.

Cover the filling with the crumble in an even layer. Bake, uncovered, for 30 minutes, then cover with foil and return to the oven for a further 15 minutes. The sides should be bubbling a bit and the fruit soft. If it needs a little extra time, pop it back in for another 15 minutes.

Serve warm or hot with a scoop of ice cream or coconut yoghurt. Chilled coconut cream will work at a pinch, too.

**TIPS & SWAPS**

- For an apple crumble without the rhubarb, use another few apples and omit the coconut sugar for less sweetness.
- If you don't have a food processor for making the crumble, roughly chop the nuts and seeds by hand, then combine with the other ingredients in a mixing bowl.

# SOULFUL CHAI

**PREP** 10 minutes for the spice blend, plus 10 minutes for the chai

**MAKES** about 30 servings

I've waited a long time to experience the perfect blend of spices for a chai (there's a bit of an art to getting it right). I can confirm this recipe is truly a delight and I cannot recommend it enough. Oh, your life will be enriched. And if you're already a fan of ordering the odd chai at your local coffee spot, you'll be chuffed when you realise you can make one just as good (well, better actually) at home. Each sip feels like a joyous, satisfying balance of spice, warmth and earthiness – real nourishment for the soul. If you can, look for fresh (and ideally even organic) spices, I reckon it does make a difference! I wouldn't be without my frother for the milk, but it's not essential. Did you know you can froth hot milk in a plunger, too? Just pump the filter thing up and down a few times and boom!

### CHAI SPICE BLEND

3 tbsp ground cinnamon

3 tbsp ground ginger

1½ tbsp ground cardamom

1½ tsp ground nutmeg

1½ tsp allspice

¾ tsp fine black pepper

1 vanilla bean pod (optional)

### TO SERVE (PER PERSON)

1 cup milk (plant-based if preferred)

1 tsp Chai Spice Blend

2 tsp coconut sugar, agave syrup or maple syrup, plus extra if desired

To make the chai spice blend, combine the ground spices and pepper in a bowl and mix with a small whisk or fork until well combined.

Transfer to an airtight glass canister or jar and add the vanilla pod (if using). It will store well in a cool, dark place for several months.

To prepare your chai, warm the milk in a saucepan over a medium heat. Add the chai spice blend and sugar or syrup and stir for a few minutes with a whisk until frothy and hot (don't let it boil). Sprinkle with a little extra sugar or syrup if you like.

Either take a moment of peace for yourself in a patch of sunlight with your chai, or share with someone you adore.

### TIPS & SWAPS

- I find 1 tsp Chai Spice Blend to 1 cup milk and 2 tsp sweetener is a good balanced ratio, but if you enjoy it a little spicier try using 1½ tsp Chai Spice Blend and adjusting the sweetener to suit.
- An alternative for sweetening your chai is to add 4 dates per person to the milk mixture in the saucepan. Once it's hot, for an extra creamy and frothy experience whizz everything together in a blender until smooth. You may need to reheat the chai in the saucepan afterwards.
- If you have a milk frother, you can froth a little extra milk to dollop on top of the chai.
- Adding 1-2 tbsp of full-fat coconut cream to the milk mixture makes it extra decadent.
- Adding a tiny pinch of salt takes it to another level.

# BITS & BOBS

# HEMP & CORIANDER PESTO

**PREP** 15 minutes
**MAKES** about 2 cups

⅔ cup hemp seeds or hearts
⅓ cup nutritional yeast flakes
2 large cloves garlic
1½ tsp salt
½ tsp fine black pepper
2 cups tightly packed roughly chopped fresh coriander leaves and stalks
1¼ cups basil leaves or roughly chopped fresh parsley
¼ cup fresh lemon juice
¾ cup extra virgin olive oil

And so continues my healthy obsession with the humble hemp seed (see page 226), here in the form of pesto. In the past I've used pine nuts, cashews and sunflower seeds as the creamy element in my pesto, but I had an inkling hemp would be a whole new fabulous thing and it did not disappoint. These wonderful seeds add a nutty, earthy flavour of their own that the coriander holds up well against. I use this on everything, from toast to Mexican food, tossed through pasta or cooked potatoes, on a platter or anywhere you'd normally use a pesto. It's fresh and vibrant and a good deal nicer than most of the store-bought ones, I promise.

Place the hemp, yeast flakes, garlic, salt and pepper in a food processor and whizz to a fine crumb.

Add the herbs and lemon juice and pulse until minced, scraping down the sides as necessary.

With the motor running, add the olive oil in a medium stream until all incorporated. Scrape down the sides to get it all together.

Check the flavours and season with more salt and lemon if you think it needs it. It should taste balanced and pop with flavour (it might start off quite intense and even a little bitter, but it mellows out in the fridge after a day).

Store in a sealed jar or container in the fridge for up to a week.

TIPS & SWAPS

- If you have a set of scales and want to get a more accurate measure of the herbs, you'll need 60g (2¼ oz) fresh coriander leaves and stalks, and 50g (1¾ oz) basil leaves or roughly chopped parsley.

# SOFT HERBY CHEESE

**PREP** 15 minutes
**MAKES** about 1½ cups

1 cup raw cashews
2 cups water
6 tbsp nutritional yeast flakes
2 tbsp lemon juice
1 tbsp cornflour
1 tbsp vegetable stock powder
1 tbsp agar-agar powder
1 tsp maple syrup
1 clove garlic, peeled
¾ tsp salt
⅛ tsp fine white pepper
⅛ tsp fine black pepper
8 fresh basil leaves
⅓ cup roughly chopped fresh soft herbs, such as dill, parsley and chives
1 tsp chopped hard herbs, such as rosemary and thyme leaves (optional)

**TO SERVE (OPTIONAL)**

extra thyme sprigs
toast or crackers

Who knew it was this easy to whip up such a sensationally tasty and moreish dairy-free cheese? Simply blend, heat and pour. It's very much reminiscent of Boursin, the famous French herbed soft cheese, and let me tell you that is no bad thing. The agar-agar powder helps it firm up to a cheese-like consistency, but it remains soft enough to smush. It's fabulous smeared on fresh crusty bread, crackers or even toast with sliced tomatoes on top, and it's great in sandwiches, too!

Lightly grease two 300–400ml (10½–14 fl oz) ramekins or glass dishes with olive oil.

If you have a powerful blender, you don't need to soak the cashews. If you're unsure, soak them in just-boiled water for 20 minutes first, then drain.

Add everything except the herbs to a blender or bullet and whizz on high speed for a minute, or until silky smooth.

Add the herbs and pulse a couple of times – you want them chopped but not fully blended or the cheese will be too green.

Pour into a medium saucepan over a medium heat and stir continuously until the mixture bubbles and thickens up – a few minutes at least. Cook for another 2 minutes once it's thickened to make sure the agar-agar has been activated.

Check the flavours and season with salt if you think it needs it. Keep in mind the salt level will decrease slightly as it cools.

Divide between the prepared dishes, cover and refrigerate for at least 2 hours until it has firmed up nicely. It will keep in the fridge for a week.

Serve turned out onto a platter or cheese board, garnished with the thyme and accompanied by thin oiled toast or crackers. Dig in and enjoy!

### TIPS & SWAPS

- Agar-agar powder is a flavourless, odourless powder derived from a type of algae (sounds gross but isn't). It's used for many things, but especially as a plant-based alternative to gelatine in cooking, baking and desserts. Here, it helps the cheese set to a consistency you can slice, which feels more authentic. You can usually find agar-agar powder at your local supermarket, greengrocer or specialty store.

# FANCY PATÉ

**PREP** 20 minutes, plus 2+ hours setting time
**COOK** 25 minutes
**MAKES** about 1 cup

I've had a number of (quite discerning) people taste this paté and seem mildly taken aback by the fact that it's so like a traditional paté – obviously in the way it presents itself, but even the texture and the rich flavour it boasts. No need for livers, if that ain't your thing. It's a welcome addition to any kind of grazing or entertaining platter, or perfect served by itself on mini toasts, crackers or crostini when you want a mouthwatering little morsel with a glass of something chilled. In other words, when a bag of chips and a punnet of dip simply won't do.

### PATÉ

- 6 tbsp plant-based butter or refined coconut oil
- 2 large shallots, sliced (about ½ cup)
- 250g (9 oz) brown button mushrooms, thinly sliced
- 3 cloves garlic, finely chopped
- 1 tsp fresh thyme leaves
- ¾ cup roughly chopped walnuts
- 1 tbsp balsamic vinegar
- 1 tbsp white (shiro) miso paste
- ½ tsp salt
- ¼ tsp fine black pepper

### TOPPING

- ⅓ cup apricot jam (sugar-free if preferred)
- 2 tsp cornflour mixed with 2 tbsp water
- 2 tsp lemon juice
- ¼ tsp mixed spice

### TO SERVE (OPTIONAL)

- crackers, crostini or bread of your choice
- pickles, olives and cheeses (plant-based if preferred)

To make the paté, melt half the butter or oil in a pan over a medium-low heat. Add the shallots and cook for 6–7 minutes, stirring often, until beginning to turn golden.

Add the mushrooms, garlic, thyme and the remaining butter or oil and cook for another 7 minutes, stirring often, until fragrant and soft.

Add the walnuts and vinegar and cook for a further 3 minutes, stirring.

Remove from the heat and stir in the miso, salt and pepper. Allow to cool for about 10 minutes, then transfer to a food processor and whizz for a good 5 minutes until it's as smooth as possible. You'll need to scrape down the sides a few times as you go.

Transfer the mixture to a ramekin or smallish container, smooth the top and give the dish a bang on the chopping board to knock out any air pockets. Top with a little cracked pepper, cover and refrigerate until cold.

To make the fruity topping, combine all the ingredients in a small saucepan over a medium heat. Simmer for a couple of minutes, stirring, until thickened and clear. Check the flavours and season to taste with salt and pepper. Remove from the heat and allow to cool for a few minutes.

When the topping has cooled, pour it over the paté and refrigerate for a couple of hours until set.

Serve with crackers, crostini or bread, accompanied by pickles, olives and your favourite cheeses.

### TIPS & SWAPS

- To make an even easier topping, you can melt down fruit paste (the one you'd put on a cheeseboard) with a splash of water and pour it on top of the pate before refrigerating to set.
- Refined coconut oil is a flavourless oil that's able to tolerate high heat. It might be labelled 'coconut cooking oil' at the supermarket.

# SEEMINGLY SMOKED SALMON

**PREP** 1 hour 15 minutes, plus 6+ hours marinating time

**SERVES** 4 as a snack

- 5 medium (400g / 14 oz) carrots (I like organic)
- ½ large sheet nori (sushi seaweed) or a few smaller snack-sized sheets

**MARINADE**

- 5 tbsp lemon juice
- 4 tbsp grapeseed or sunflower oil
- 1½ tbsp capers, drained and roughly chopped
- 1½ tbsp caper brine from the jar
- 1 tbsp maple syrup
- 1 tsp dried dill or 1–2 tbsp finely chopped fresh dill
- ½ tsp liquid smoke (optional, but kind of not optional; see page 226)
- ½ tsp salt
- ¼ tsp fine black or white pepper

**TO SERVE (OPTIONAL)**

- bagels, crackers or toast
- plant-based cream cheese or avocado
- finely sliced red onion or tomato
- capers
- fresh dill
- lemon juice

**It looks undeniably like smoked salmon. But yeah, that's definitely carrot. How can this humble root vegetable keep giving us so much? (You know you all loved the carrot Not Dogs in *Supergood*.) This is a fabulous recipe, so lovely to eat and also worth making for the sheer novelty factor of it, and the look on people's faces when they try it. It really does taste like you're eating smoked salmon because the nori (sushi seaweed) in the marinade gives it the inimitable flavour of the sea. Add in those beloved classics like dill, lemon and capers and of course that magical liquid smoke, and suddenly your mouth is telling you one thing but your brain another. And that's a sign it's worked!**

Preheat the oven to 200°C (400°F) regular bake and have a medium roasting tray ready.

Peel the carrots, then wrap in foil and place on the baking tray. Bake for 45 minutes, then remove from the oven and set aside until cooled right down.

Using a sharp knife or peeler, slice the carrots lengthways as thinly as possible. It helps if you shave a thin piece off one side of the carrot to hold it steady while you chop.

Chop the nori into tiny pieces.

To make the marinade, combine the ingredients in a container big enough to hold the carrots (I use a glass one with a sealed lid). Add the nori and stir to combine. Add the carrots and toss gently to coat evenly. Cover and refrigerate for at least 6 hours or up to a week, to let all the flavours infuse (carefully stir it once if you remember).

When ready to serve, simply pick the pieces of carrot from the dish and use them – don't rinse them! The little pieces of nori are yummy to eat as well.

Serve on crackers, bagels or toast, with your choice of cream cheese or avo, red onion or tomato, capers and fresh dill. An extra crack of pepper, sprinkle of salt and squeeze of lemon is nice, too.

# PITA BREADS

**PREP** 1 hour, plus 1 hour 30 minutes rising time

**COOK** 30 minutes

**MAKES** 8

- 350g (12 oz) plain white flour
- 150g (5½ oz) wholemeal flour
- 1 tsp salt
- 2 tbsp extra virgin olive oil or grapeseed oil
- 300ml (10½ fl oz) warm water (about skin temperature or 40°C (100°F))
- 2 tsp active yeast granules (check expiry date)
- 1 tsp coconut sugar

**This particular recipe isn't gluten-free, but I just had to share it. I bet you didn't realise how painless it was to make pita bread that turns out just like store-bought, but even nicer coz it's fresh! So how do you get that little pocket in there? Just prepare a regular bread-like dough, then all it takes is a super-hot pizza stone in the oven (or a cast-iron pan, at a pinch) and poof! They look awesome when they cook, puffing up like adorable little bread balloons. A must-watch (just like *Ted Lasso*). Serve stuffed with falafel (see page 46) and tahini sauce or any other tasty filling, or use as a dipper with olive oil, hummus or other dips. They're great in lunchboxes, and after a day they're good heated up in the oven or toaster — or cut up and baked into little crackers for a platter.**

Combine the flours and salt in a large mixing bowl. Make a well in the centre and add the oil. Set aside.

Place the warm water, yeast and coconut sugar in a jug or bowl and whisk for a few seconds. Set aside for 5–10 minutes to activate the yeast until it 'blooms' (goes a bit puffy and rises to the top).

Add the yeasty water to the flour bowl and bring the dough together into a craggy mass. Turn onto a clean benchtop and knead for 8–10 minutes — you should be sweating by the end and the dough should be soft and silky and stretchy. It's ready when you can stretch a small piece until it becomes translucent. You can knead it for a few minutes using the dough hook in your stand mixer if you prefer, but I like doing it by hand.

Rinse and lightly oil the bowl you mixed the flour in. Make the dough into a ball and place it in the bowl. Cover with a clean, damp tea towel and put it somewhere warm (like a hot water cupboard, or in the turned-off oven with a mug of just-boiled water inside) until the dough has doubled in size. If it doesn't spring back when you poke it with your finger, you're ready for the next step!

Preheat the oven to 250°C (500°F) fan bake (or as high as your oven will go). Place a pizza stone or cast-iron pan in the lower half of the oven to preheat.

Divide the dough into 8 pieces and roll into rough ball shapes.

Roll out your first ball of dough on a lightly floured surface to make a 15cm (6 in) disc that's about 3mm (⅛ in) thick. Take care not to rip the dough or leave creases.

Repeat with the remaining balls, then arrange them on a lightly floured benchtop. Cover with a clean, damp tea towel and leave for 20–30 minutes to puff slightly.

By now your oven should have been up to temperature for at least 15 minutes. If not, wait until it has.

Take the first pita bread and place the side that was face up, face down on the hot pizza stone in the oven. Eventually it will start to puff up into a balloon. It's cooked when it reaches a full, spherical puff, which should take 2–3 minutes (they don't need to fully brown). If it doesn't puff up, or only partially puffs, don't worry, it will still taste great. Check the tips to the left, and you'll be getting consistent puff before you know it!

Place the cooked pita on a dish and cover with a clean, damp tea towel while you repeat to cook the rest.

### TIPS & SWAPS

- If you're using 'instant' yeast rather than active, you don't need to 'bloom' it first.
- The dough can be prepared ahead of time and left to double in size (proof) twice, knocking it back down after each time. It can then be covered with clingfilm and refrigerated for up to 24 hours.
- A very hot oven and cooking surface is key to making pitas puff up. Minimise the time you leave the oven door open and let the oven return to full heat between pitas. A pizza stone is an ideal cooking surface because it can store a large amount of heat.
- The air pocket forms when water in the bread turns into steam, so always keep your dough covered with a clean, damp tea towel to prevent it drying out.
- Be careful to avoid creases or tears in the dough and try not to use too much flour for dusting.

# JUNGLE CURRY PASTE

**PREP** 10 minutes
**MAKES** about 1 cup

3 shallots, peeled
6 cloves garlic, peeled
1 large red chilli, deseeded
½ cup chopped fresh coriander leaves and stalks
¼ cup raw almonds or cashews
¼ cup sesame oil
3 tbsp soy sauce or tamari
2–3 tbsp sriracha
2 tbsp coconut sugar or maple syrup
4 tsp whole coriander seeds
1 tbsp salt
1 tsp ground turmeric
3 fresh makrut lime leaves or zest of 2 large lemons or 3 limes
juice of 1 lemon or lime

This is a very exciting recipe. It's a powerhouse of flavour, it's versatile, it's simple to make and it's going to change your life! If I sound like a highly charged motivational speaker it's because recipes like this light me up. I love the ease of having a jar on hand, with which you can make magic at the drop of a hat. Try it out in a very special fried-rice dish (see page 34) or roasted cauliflower salad (see page 126). After that, just get creative with it. Marinate your favourite skewers then barbecue them. Fry it up as a curry paste and add your favourite protein, veges and coconut milk. Just don't serve it raw – it needs to be cooked to mellow it out.

Place all the ingredients in a bullet or small food processor. Whizz until you have a thin paste (it doesn't have to be totally smooth), scraping down the sides to make sure it's all incorporated.

Transfer to a glass jar or well-sealed container. It will keep for a few weeks in the fridge, or a couple of months in the freezer, tightly sealed.

### TIPS & SWAPS

- For a milder, child-friendly version, leave out the sriracha.
- For a nut-free version, replace the almonds or cashews with sunflower seeds.
- Makrut lime leaves (also known as kaffir lime leaves) are one of my true loves. They have a beautifully fragrant citrus smell and a fresh, aromatic lemony flavour. You can get them from the supermarket.

# CORIANDER CHUTNEY

**PREP** 10 minutes
**MAKES** about 1 cup

This is a fresh, tangy, spicy and vibrant condiment that adds a whole new level of deliciousness to Indian-style dishes (and there are a fair few of those in this book!). It kind of feels like less of a chutney and more of a little sauce, but still. It takes just minutes to prepare and looks great on the table. Dollop on and enjoy!

- 3 cups (70g / 2½ oz) coriander leaves and stalks
- ¼ cup roasted peanuts, roasted cashews or raw hemp seeds
- 2 large green chillies, deseeded
- 1 tbsp chopped fresh ginger
- 2–3 large cloves garlic
- 2 tbsp lemon juice
- 2 tsp maple syrup
- 1½ tsp roasted ground cumin (or cumin seeds toasted in a dry pan until fragrant)
- ¾ tsp salt, or to taste

Place all the ingredients in a bullet or small food processor and whizz until smooth, scraping down the sides a couple of times. Add more salt if it needs it.

It will last for a few days in a jar in the fridge.

### TIPS & SWAPS

- Roasted ground cumin (also known as roasted cumin powder or bhuna jeera powder) has a more intense flavour than standard ground cumin. You can find it at some supermarkets, specialty stores or online stores.

# CHERMOULA

**PREP** 10 minutes
**MAKES** about 1 cup

- 1 cup (30g / 1 oz) fresh coriander leaves and stalks
- 1 cup (40g / 1½ oz) roughly chopped flat-leaf parsley
- 1 cup (10g / ¼ oz) fresh mint leaves
- ½ cup good-quality extra virgin olive oil
- ½ cup fresh lemon juice
- 3 wedges preserved lemon (optional but extraordinary)
- 6 cloves garlic, peeled
- 1 tbsp maple syrup
- 2 tbsp ground cumin
- 1½ tbsp smoked paprika
- 2 tsp ground coriander
- 2 tsp salt
- 1 tsp fine black pepper
- pinch chilli flakes

A Moroccan-inspired version of the traditional North African condiment, this chermoula is a delicious blend of fresh aromatic herbs, garlic, earthy spices and zingy lemon (if you can find preserved lemon, it adds a whole other dimension). Traditionally used to flavour fish and seafood, nowadays it's perhaps the most versatile little number you could have lurking in your fridge because its uses are seemingly endless – and the flavour it adds to a simple dish is phenomenal. Use it as a marinade or a sauce for grilled meat, seafood or tofu. Stir it through the lentil soup on page 20, use it as a dressing on a salad of grilled summer vegetables (see page 130) or toss it through hot pasta. Swirl a spoonful through plain yoghurt or hummus, or use it neat as a dip on a platter. Drizzle sparingly on avocado toast, spread lightly in a sandwich, or spread on crusty flatbread with whatever topping you please. As you can see, a world of pleasure awaits you, so get whizzing! Thank you to the lovely Malika for this life-changing recipe.

Place all the ingredients in a food processor and whizz until smooth, scraping down the sides as you go.

Store in an airtight jar in the fridge for up to two weeks – the vibrancy of the colour may fade, but the flavours will get better with time.

### TIPS & SWAPS

- You can halve the quantities for a smaller batch if you don't need a whole lot.
- If you can't find preserved lemons, use the zest of 2–3 fresh lemons instead.

# SMOKED AÏOLI

**PREP** 5 minutes
**MAKES** about 1 cup

- 1 recipe plant-based aïoli (see my website or *Supergood*) or 1 cup store-bought mayo (vegan if preferred)
- 2 tsp mild or sweet smoked paprika
- 2 tsp maple syrup
- 2 tsp lemon juice
- ¼ tsp liquid smoke (see page 226)

I have it on good authority that once you try this kick-ass little condiment, you'll realise that you can slather it on an enormous variety of savoury things and make them infinitely more delicious (think potato wedges, as a starting point). It totally tastes like bacon-flavoured mayonnaise, but it's plant-based. Um, how much more do you need to know? And if I haven't yet convinced you that your pantry needs a bottle of natural liquid smoke sitting in it always, this is another sign. Go online and do it!

Combine all the ingredients in a bowl and mix well. If it's too thick for your liking, add a little soy milk, water or lemon juice to thin it down.

It will keep in a sealed jar or container in the fridge for a week.

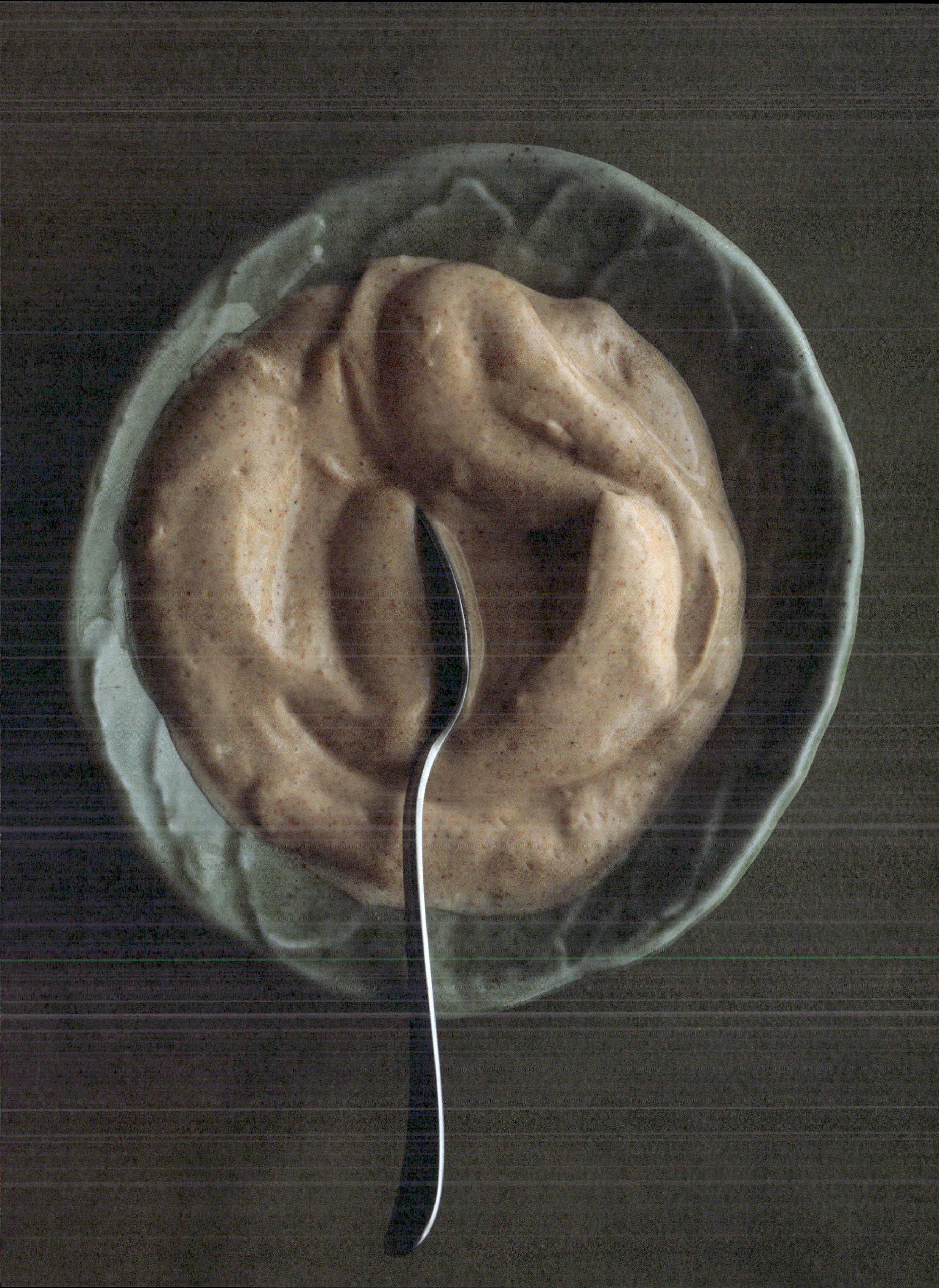

# GLUTEN-FREE FLOUR BLEND

**PREP** 15 minutes
**MAKES** 5 cups

3 cups brown rice flour
1 cup potato starch (or cornflour)
½ cup white rice flour
½ cup tapioca flour (or arrowroot flour)
2 tsp xanthan gum (see page 227)

This blend has transformed my gluten-free baking game. It's designed for light baking, such as cakes, slices, cookies, muffins and sweet loaves. In other words, it's not going to miraculously produce a loaf of crusty bread, naan or pizza dough (although you can find my recipe for gluten-free pizza dough on page 32). It's a staple in my pantry, I use it more often than regular flour and many of the baking recipes in this book have been tested with it. I can't overemphasise how much better it performs than store-bought blends (which seem to consist mostly of cornstarch). You can order the ingredients online (that's what I do, in bulk) or you'll easily find them at a specialty food store, wholefoods store or bulk foods refillery. The result is worth the small amount of effort if you care about the texture of your baking — which you totally should! I usually double the quantities and make a big batch, since I use a lot of it.

Add all the ingredients to a large sealable container and shake well to combine.

Store well-sealed in a cool, dark place and use within 6 months.

### TIPS & SWAPS

- You can find xanthan gum in good supermarkets, health stores, specialty food stores and bulk food stores, or buy it online. It's crucial for gluten-free baking, as it helps provide the structure that's missing with the absence of gluten.
- Tapioca flour is also known as tapioca starch. You can use arrowroot flour (also called arrowroot powder and arrowroot starch) in its place if you have to and the result will still be good.
- Try to use the ingredients that I've listed first; if you can't get them, sub in the bracketed ones.

# INGREDIENTS TO GET EXCITED ABOUT

Following on from the 'Say hello to your new friends' section in *Supergood*, allow me to introduce a handsome new lineup of kitchen superstars who all deserve recognition for their valiant efforts in raising the bar of plant-based cooking! Some of them may be completely new to you, and some you may have used in different ways. Most of them are easy enough to source, and all of them add something very special to this book to help make it what it is.

My vibe has always been about making epic food using simple ingredients you can find at the supermarket, and that's something I'm still proud of, seven cookbooks later. I'm not a 'fancy' person and I don't use 'fancy' ingredients just to try and be, um, 'fancy'. At the same time, I do feel like I'm here to inspire new ideas, especially when they elevate a dish or lift other ingredients to scrumptious new levels (something everyone at your table will appreciate). I'm constantly learning about food from people, places and experiences, as well as through my own research and intuition – therefore my cooking is always evolving. And of course, through my own creations, I end up sharing with you the very best of what resonates and feels and tastes good. So, with this section, think of it as broadening your horizons and, ultimately, helping you take things to a new level. Let's be honest: the same old stuff all the time gets a bit bloody boring, don't you reckon? So here we go ...

## 1. HEMP SEEDS

I'm putting hemp seeds (which are technically a nut) first, because of how incredibly important they are. I could harp on all day about the myriad uses of the hemp plant and how it could *literally* save our planet, but for now let's focus on the seeds (or hearts). No, you won't get high eating them. But you *will* get super-high-quality protein (they contain all the essential amino acids, making them a complete protein source), omega-3 and omega-6, good fats, and an impressive array of vitamins and minerals including iron, zinc, vitamin E, magnesium, potassium and B vitamins. On top of all that, they're yummy — creamy, nutty, delicious. Eat them every day. Dry-toast them in a pan until golden and sprinkle on salads or savoury meals. Use them raw in smoothies (I do this for my kids daily) or in muesli or baking. I've created for you a delicious Hemp & Coriander Pesto (page 202), a tasty Veg-Out Macaroni Cheese (page 88), a wholesome Apple & Rhubarb Crumble (page 196) and a brilliantly fresh Creamy Herb Dressing (page 118) — all of which use these beauties. When it comes to hemp seeds, I buy a big bag in bulk and make sure I never run out.

## 2. SALT

I simply must include a note about salt in all of my books now, for newcomers (or those of you who missed the memo last time), because salt is important. When I'm testing my recipes and checking the salt level, I use either fine Himalayan salt or fine sea salt (I also really love Celtic sea salt). Using the standard, superfine iodised table salt will give you a different (saltier) result than mine, and personally I don't use it. Flaky sea salt is lovely for finishing a plate of food but, again, I wouldn't use that when measuring salt for a recipe.

## 3. LIQUID SMOKE

A little bottle of natural liquid smoke is something I reckon everyone should have in their pantry. This stuff is magic! It's basically a liquid that's been infused with real smoke then condensed, and it's perfect for adding a delicious smoked, bacony or grilled-BBQ flavour to food. Best of all, a bottle will last you ages because you only need a tiny amount each time. Some lovely natural varieties are quickly becoming available in good supermarkets, as well as in most specialty food stores or online. Liquid smoke makes the Smoky Pea Soup (page 42) and Fush Pie (page 78) in this book SING with heavenly flavour. Don't forget the Smoked Aïoli (page 220) either!

## 4. CHICKPEA FLOUR

Chickpea flour is SUCH a superstar. How did I only start using it in my late 30s? A staple in traditional Indian cuisine, it's a gluten-free flour that magically behaves in a similar way to eggs when it's used in a batter or fritter mixture, tart or quiche. It also works as a thickener or binding agent, or as part of a gluten-free flour mixture. I'm hooked on using it in my Crêpelettes (page 62) and Bigbog Brownies (page 136).

Standard chickpea flour is made from ground-up dried kabuli chickpeas. There are other chickpea flours, such as besan (also known as gram flour) — essentially besan is made using a different kind of chickpea (desi), which is darker and stronger and will behave slightly differently in recipes. For the recipes in this book I've used standard chickpea flour, which is lighter and fluffier. You can find it at most supermarkets now, which is a cause to celebrate.

## 5. MISO PASTE

Miso paste, a traditional Japanese seasoning, is another one of our flavour heroes because it gives us that all-important 'umami' flavour we Kiwis so love in our meals (especially useful for the meatless ones). Essentially, it's a thick paste made by fermenting soybeans — we've all seen the delicious clouds that billow up from it in a cup of miso soup. I've used it, of course, in the Mushroomy Miso Noodle Soup (page 104), but you'll see it featuring in loads of my other recipes. That's because a small amount added to a dish gives a 'tasty' (see what I did there) depth of flavour that makes you salivate while you eat it. Too much, and it'll taste weird. But the right amount can be just that little something your meat-free meal might otherwise be missing. All supermarkets stock it.

## 6. TEMPEH

Tempeh is a traditional Indonesian food made from cultured and fermented soybeans that end up bound in the form of a hard, dense cake. When thinly sliced, it crisps up beautifully if you fry it well (as in the Sushi Bowls on page 98), and it also happily absorbs the flavours of whatever sauce you're serving it with (you either want to marinate it first, or have something to douse it in after cooking). Because the soybeans have been fermented, the soy protein is easier on the gut, and because whole beans are used in the process, tempeh contains more fibre than tofu. It's also a great source of protein, prebiotics, and a wide array of vitamins and minerals. More of this little gem to come in the future! It's available in all supermarkets.

## 7. STOCK POWDER

I'm in no way getting paid to say this, but I feel obliged to share because it's a game changer when I'm in plant-based cooking mode: I generally use Massel stock cubes for my recipes. There are several flavours available, they're all plant-based, and *man* they add a truly remarkable flavour. I don't know how they do it (maybe I don't want to know), but I'm here for it. As a guide, I find that two teaspoons of regular stock powder is the equivalent of one Massel cube. You can find them in all supermarkets, either as cubes packed in a thin box or as tins of powder. Other brands of stock powder will work just as well, though (look for the organic ones).

## 8. SRIRACHA

Sriracha is a garlicky chilli sauce, originating from Thailand and made from a paste of chillies, garlic, vinegar, sugar and salt. It gives savoury dishes an extra flavour boost – plus a nice little kick of heat – without you having to do any extra legwork. I always have a bottle in the fridge because it goes in (and on) a lot of things: stir-fries, burgers, eggs, sandwiches, soups. You can also use it as a dipping sauce (the Spring Rolls on page 86 would love it). It's a lot milder than, say, Tabasco, which is why it's so popular: the spice level is just right for the average person's spice tolerance. It's still a hot chilli sauce, but it's mild enough that most of us can taste and enjoy its flavours rather than just getting blasted with heat.

## 9. XANTHAN GUM

This is the secret to gluten-free baking, and a key ingredient in my Gluten-Free Flour Blend (page 222), Gluten-Free Pizza (page 32) and Gluten-Free Fruit Toast (page 170). It helps to replace the structure and texture that's missing when gluten isn't present, and stops things ending up a dense, stodgy mess. A little bit of xanthan gum helps muffins to stay puffed-up and cakes to rise proudly. A little bit more helps to create gluten-free pizza dough and gluten-free breads. Seeing it's become so popular, you can now find it in the spice aisle of good supermarkets, as well as in health stores, specialty stores and refilleries. While it's technically derived from a plant, you wouldn't exactly call it a 'health food', but I don't mind using it every now and then in home baking.

## 10. TAHINI

Tahini is simply a paste made from roasted sesame seeds. Most people know it as something you put in hummus, but its uses far surpass that. I love it so much because it adds a sumptuous creamy element to certain dishes without having to resort to mayo (I still love mayo, but remember we are broadening horizons here). I also love it because it's full of healthy fats and rich in antioxidants, with anti-inflammatory properties to boot. Try to find the unhulled version, as the kind that includes the ground-up seed husks can be a little bitter. When I use it, I always balance it out with salt, lemon and maple syrup to make it delicious.

## 11. TEXTURED SOY PROTEIN

It feels like you're eating mince, but this ain't mince. For me, textured soy protein (also called textured vegetable protein or TVP) is the only thing that does the job of achieving that real meaty chewiness that nothing else can quite imitate. It's both cheap and easy to prepare; just rehydrate it in liquid stock and cook it like you would mince. You *will* need to add a load of extra flavours because TSP soaks them all up, big time. I've got you covered with my Mince & Cheese Pie (page 48) and Meatballs & Gravy (page 30), but you can also try it in lasagne, Mexican chilli, burger patties, stir-fries, Bolognese, cottage pie – you get the gist. The best part is that it's made from dehydrated soy protein and that's all; no other added nasties. It's a good source of protein and fibre, too. I buy it from my local supermarket, and I love to use it occasionally as part of a balanced approach to protein sources.

## 12. CACAO BUTTER

I've only used this ingredient in one recipe (the Mint-As Slice on page 144), but it deserves a mention because it really is quite wonderful – and you'll be seeing more of it. Cacao butter is a natural fat extracted from cacao beans (nothing to do with actual butter), and it's a great dairy-free option for adding a luscious, creamy, chocolatey vibe to homemade chocolate, baking or desserts – and even skincare. It has a beautiful aroma but is very mild in flavour. For me, using cacao butter was the perfect way to get my slice to set without using butter or icing sugar. And, of course, the decadence it provides is utter heaven. It's *well* worth seeking out at good supermarkets, your local specialty or organic store, refilleries or online stores. It's a 'sometimes' thing because it's not exactly cheap ... but, honestly, what is these days?

2
5
1
6
10

3
4
7
11
12
8
9

# LOVE & GRATITUDE

Let me tell you, this book simply couldn't have come into being without a number of truly magnificent people — mainly women, actually — coming together and bringing their A game (and big hearts) with it.

But first up I've just actually gotta thank life itself — this magical process of constant creation. I'm in love with you, life! Every day is like a pinch-me moment (sounds like a worn-out cliché but it's very real). Sure, there are ups and downs, and challenging moments when I lose the plot. But I'm truly happy to be here, present in this moment, doing exactly this.

I'm also eternally thankful for **you, my readers and fellow home cooks**. You're a hugely important part of my life. We're connected, you and I, whether you like it or not! Thank you for trusting me in your kitchens as you nourish your loved ones — you're the reason I'm doing this, and your support means everything.

**Jenny, Leanne, Mads, Mel, Abba, Grace, Jane, and my extraordinarily talented team at Allen & Unwin**. Such awesome people. Thank you for trusting me with my dream and giving me free reign to gallop off with it (that's the only way I roll). Everyone involved has put in a tremendous amount of inspired and very hard work behind the scenes to help *Tasty* reach its highest potential and to make it the roaring success it is. I never take that for granted, and I'm extremely grateful for every one of you. You've made the process a seamless and enjoyable one for me.

**Tam and Vic**. People might think what you do is all snapping a camera and arranging lovely props, when in reality it's something monumentally more important and beautifully complex. You two have been co-creating the very heart and soul of my books with me since the beginning. Your combined vision is divine; your talent at bringing it to life as inspired individuals is synergy at its finest. I know you care deeply for this book. And for me, and for my boys ... and it shows. I love you both, so very much.

To the astounding **Heliena** — you're a blessing to this world, and to me, through every facet of your radiant being. *Tasty* wouldn't be what it is without you. I love you endlessly, always. Thank you.

**Jenny McKinnon**, you remarkable woman. You so beautifully and diligently keep everything flowing in the way it needs to so that I can do what I do best. Details aren't always my cherished friend, but I'm sure grateful that you are! I love you, and thank you. And **Gibby** — soul brother — I love you, too.

**Belinda**, toiling on my behalf behind the scenes, with utter dedication and integrity always; alongside me for 11 years and counting! I love you, and thank you.

**Becky**, when is a nanny not a nanny? When she's like a sister! You are the gift of gifts. Helping me with my little scamps; a true embodiment of love, compassion and care. You're a treasured part of my family I could not imagine being without. I love you, thank you.

**Auh, Maumau**! (Andrea). Alongside me for the entire creation of this book. It may have been via Whatsapp, but you were making me laugh, every day, all day. My god, you're wildly clever beyond comprehension (and have the heart to match). Everything is energy, and that joy went straight into the food on every page — everyone should be on their knees thanking you, just as I am now. Puhleeease!

My phenomenal **Mum** — for helping with the kids, but mostly for a lifetime of encouraging me to shine.

And to my beloved family and close friends: you all know who you are, but I'll run out of room if I keep rambling on — know that I adore you and I'm beyond grateful to have you in my life.

Also ... I can't create without music. So thanks to Keith Urban, Sam Hunt, Thomas Rhett, Kacey Musgraves and all the other excellent artists who got me through some very loooong days of cooking. (Yeah, so *Tasty* coincided with a pretty solid country music phase. That happened!)

# INDEX

## N



## O



## P



## R



## S

## T



## V



## W



## Z

Chelsea uses New Zealand standard measures, including the 15ml (3 teaspoon) tablespoon. If you are using the Australian 20ml (4 teaspoon) tablespoon, you may wish to remove a teaspoon of ingredient for each tablespoon specified.

First published in 2024



Creative direction by Tamara West
Design by Madeleine Kane
Styling by Victoria Bell



Allen & Unwin
Level 2, 10 College Hill, Freemans Bay
Auckland 1011, New Zealand
+64 (9) 377 3800
auckland@allenandunwin.com
www.allenandunwin.co.nz

83 Alexander Street
Crows Nest NSW 2065, Australia
+61 (2) 8425 0100

A catalogue record for this book is available from the National Library of New Zealand.

ISBN 978 1 991006 51 6

Printed in China by 1010 Printing Limited

10 9 8 7 6 5 4 3 2 1

MIX
Paper | Supporting responsible forestry
FSC® C016973